1 MONTH OF
FREE
READING

at
www.ForgottenBooks.com

By purchasing this book you are eligible for one month membership to ForgottenBooks.com, giving you unlimited access to our entire collection of over 1,000,000 titles via our web site and mobile apps.

To claim your free month visit:

www.forgottenbooks.com/free961403

ISBN 978-0-260-64088-8
PIBN 10961403

THE WORLD AGRICULTURAL SITUATION

CONTENTS

Approved by
The World Food and Agricultural Outlook
and Situation Board
and Summary released
June 21, 1977

Situation Coordinator:
Richard M. Kennedy
202-447-8260

Foreign Demand and Competition Division
Economic Research Service
U.S. Department of Agriculture
Washington, D.C. 20250

The *World Agricultural Situation* is published in June, September, and December. Agricultural situation reports for the world's major regions are published during March-May.

SUMMARY

The world buildup of large grain supplies, particularly of wheat, and early indications that large supplies will likely continue in 1977/78 remain the most prominent features of the world agricultural situation. As a result, grain prices and the volume of world grain trade are at substantially lower levels in 1976/77 than a year earlier.

The demand for imported agricultural commodities has been bolstered by the continuation of the broad-based recovery in world economic activity. However, widening imbalances in international payments and rising debt burdens cast a shadow on the longer term economic prospects for many countries.

The value of U.S. agricultural exports now seems likely to reach a record $24 billion in fiscal 1977, more than $1 billion above fiscal 1976, reflecting higher average prices but little change in volume. The U.S. agricultural trade surplus, however, will probably decline around $2 billion from the $12¼ billion of fiscal 1976 because of an expected 30-percent gain in the value of agricultural imports. Although U.S. beginning stocks are much larger than a year earlier for most commodities, except oilseeds and cotton, the value of U.S. agricultural exports may decline somewhat in fiscal 1978 if world crop conditions continue favorable during the rest of the current growing season.

Bumper 1976/77 world grain crops have reversed the tight supply conditions of the previous 3 or 4 years. But despite record availabilities, grain consumption remains below the trend of the past two decades for the third consecutive year because of lagging growth in feed grain usage in the developed countries with large feed-livestock sectors. The improved domestic supply-demand balance for grains in importing countries has contributed to a slowing of world grain trade, and a third of this year's increase in grain production is available for stock buildup. The 1976/77 carryover is expected to

Note: Unless stated otherwise, split years (e.g., 1976/77) mean July/June. Fiscal 1977 means October 1976/September 1977. Tons are metric and dollars are U.S. unless otherwise specified.

reach a 6-year high, with wheat accounting for four-fifths of the buildup. Stock increases are expected to be concentrated in a few countries—especially in the major exporting countries and the USSR. Both international and domestic grain prices—most notably wheat—have weakened and are likely to continue well below year-earlier levels.

The very preliminary data available on the 1977/78 world grain crop suggest that a crop slightly smaller than last year's 1,335 million tons is in prospect because of reduced plantings and early prospects for reduced yields due to less favorable weather. Lower grain prices relative to both 1976/77 prices and to prices of major competing crops contributed to a reduction in planted area, particularly in North America. Production estimates made this early in the year are subject to wide variations. Past experience suggests, however, that the final outcome is not likely to vary more than 5 percent in either direction from preliminary estimates in two cases out of three.

Despite some growth in both food and feed usage, 1977/78 grain consumption is expected to continue below trend and forecast production levels. Consequently, further increases in stocks seem likely—although more evenly distributed than this year among wheat and coarse grains—and only a small recovery is forecast in world grain trade, characterized by increased competition among the major exporters.

Despite the recent easing in protein meal and vegetable oil prices, the situation will continue relatively tight until new crop prospects are known. The meal situation is tighter than oil because of an unusually strong domestic and foreign demand, the short 1976 U.S. soybean crop, and a smaller-than-expected 1977 Brazilian soybean harvest. The vegetable oil situation is relatively easier than for meal, although small carryover stocks in the United States and a good domestic and strong foreign demand situation make the market sensitive to this fall's harvest.

World meat exporters continue to face heavy competition despite some slowing or leveling off of herd reductions in some countries around the world. Prospects for trade expansion also continue limited by the trade policies of major importing countries.

Dairy producer price policies and expected higher output per cow suggest that world milk production will continue to increase in 1977 at a projected 2-percent rate, compared with 1 percent in 1976. Price competition from vegetable oils has led to export subsidies in some countries to prevent further buildup in butter stocks. Large subsidies have also been granted for European Community exports of nonfat dry milk to reduce heavy stocks.

World sugar supplies remain ample as 1976/77 world production exceeded consumption. Early estimates of 1977/78 cane area show no decline because most was planted prior to the recent low prices and because of plans by several countries increased self-sufficiency or export expansion. Negotiations toward a new International Sugar Agreement were suspended in May but may be reconvened later this year.

Preliminary forecasts indicate a substantial increase in world coffee production in 1977/78, primarily because of a sharp recovery in Brazilian output from the 1975 frost, but that country's output is not likely to reach customary levels for another season or two beyond 1977/78. Prices for green coffee have declined substantially from record levels this spring.

Cocoa prices have turned upward in recent weeks, reflecting short supplies and reports of dry weather in West Africa. Major relief awaits the outcome of fall harvests.

Reduced world cotton consumption still exceeded production in 1976/77, and the 1977/78 season starts with the lowest world cotton stocks since 1953. Favorable cotton prices following 2 years of major drawdowns in stocks have prompted a substantial increase in cotton plantings for the 1977/78 season.

An expected decline in 1977 world tobacco output will face an expected increase in consumption and will result in tighter leaf supplies and firmer prices.

PAYMENTS PROBLEMS ACCOMPANY
ECONOMIC EXPANSION[1]

The broad-based recovery in world economic activity has continued even though the rate of advance slowed during the latter part of last year, and the expansion in early 1977 was somewhat

[1]This section is based on the more detailed review contained in the July 1977 *World Economic Conditions in Relation to Agricultural Trade*, WEC-12, published by the Economic Research Service.

less vigorous than a year earlier. Nevertheless, economic activity is expected to pick up and remain strong throughout the year. Some analysts project a long-awaited revival in capital investment which would strengthen aggregate demand.

The volume of world trade recovered strongly in 1976, increasing 11 to 12 percent following the decline in 1975. Projections are for a rise of 8 to 9 percent in 1977, about equal to the average growth rate over the past decade.

The trade recovery has been accompanied by widening imbalances in international payments and rising debt burdens for many countries. Together with continued world inflation these developments constrain government programs designed to stimulate growth and reduce the high unemployment levels.

At the London summit meeting in early May, the heads of the several major industrial nations reaffirmed their commitment to announced growth targets for 1977—Germany 5 percent, the United States about 6 percent, and Japan 6 to 7 percent. They declined to raise these targets, but promised to take steps that would ensure their attainment and to avoid protectionist import policies.

Most of the oil-importing countries are experiencing trade deficits. The corresponding OPEC (Organization of Petroleum Exporting Countries) surpluses are being channeled into financial institutions of a few hard currency countries and from there are then being lent to other countries with payments problems.

Although there has been limited change in the average inflation rate, developed countries fall into two distinct groups—those few hard currency countries with only moderate price rises, and those, including the United Kingdom and Italy, with serious inflationary problems.

For the developing countries, the pickup in world trade in 1976 was especially beneficial; as a group, real growth rates averaged 5 percent. The more trade oriented countries benefited from sharp increases in their exports to developed countries. Also, countries heavily dependent on agriculture generally reaped abundant harvests which brought good economic growth for the second year in a row.

Prices continued to rise sharply in most developing countries in 1976. In general, however, export prices rose more than import prices, resulting in an improvement in their foreign exchange situation. As a consequence, current account deficits declined during the year, although there was another large rise in external debt. Some modification of trade regulations and preferences in their favor were obtained in 1976 and early 1977.

Prospects are for continued economic growth in non-OPEC developing countries, but the World Bank's 1978 projections indicate per capita growth will be less than in developed countries.

Adverse trade conditions for East European countries on both the Soviet and Western markets since 1974 raised the East European debt for industrial and agricultural goods purchases in the West to $27- to $30 billion by the end of 1976. These debts cause some concern on the part of Western banks and governments as to the ability of the East European nations to attain sufficient export earnings to effect repayment.

The depressing effects of the Western recession were accompanied by a realignment in 1975 of intra-CEMA (Council for Mutual Economic Assistance) trade prices in favor of raw materials and energy, thus shifting the terms of trade to the benefit of the Soviet Union and forcing the East European nations, most of whom are poor in raw materials, to divert goods to that market. The East European response has been to restrain their borrowings as they redouble cooperative efforts to hasten a technological evolution within CEMA. At the heart of the matter is the effort to overcome the consistently poor quality of industrial output which usually keeps the East Europeans at a disadvantage in developed market countries. (*L. Jay Atkinson: 447-7590*)

WORLD PRICE DEVELOPMENTS

International commodity prices turned up this spring as short supplies of soybeans, cotton, coffee, and cocoa beans pushed prices of these commodities to record levels. In contrast, prices for grains have fallen because of plentiful supplies. Soybean prices reached $10 a bushel at the Gulf ports in April as the tight 1976/77 marketing year went into the most critical period. Recent weeks have seen a significant decline in prices of many of these commodities, especially of soybeans and coffee.

Coffee prices skyrocketed to $3.40 a pound (International Coffee Organization composite price) from the impact of the 1975 Brazilian freeze, but prices have eased significantly since mid-April. International cocoa bean prices weakened slightly

in April after climbing steadily for a year, but rose again in May.

The plentiful 1976 wheat harvest and prospects for a large 1977 wheat crop caused international wheat prices to slide 30 percent from a year ago. Corn prices dropped less because of the expected small carryover in feed grains from the 1976 crop and the general tight supply of feedstuffs emanating from the short feed supplies in Western Europe and the U.S. soybean meal situation. As a result, in recent months corn has been priced at the same or higher than wheat at Gulf ports.

Sugar prices have plunged more than 20 percent from a year ago because of large supplies. Prices for rice are 2 percent lower than a year ago while rubber is 7 percent higher.

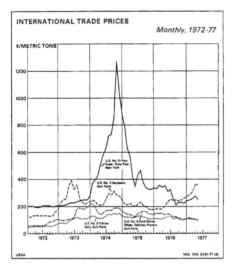

INTERNATIONAL TRADE PRICES

Monthly, 1972-77

$/METRIC TONS

USDA   NEG ERS 2491-77 (6)

Farm Prices

In May, U.S. farm prices were 2 percent higher than they were a year ago (table 1). Soybean were the leading gainers, with cotton, field peas, deciduous fruits, and wool also increasing. All the grains except rice and oats experienced falling prices, with wheat prices declining one-third. Beef cattle were priced nearly the same as last year, while hogs were 14 percent lower.

Canadian farm prices declined through December 1976, falling 10 percent from a year earlier (table 2), with declines in both the crop and livestock sectors.

Many other countries, including Japan and the EC, maintained farm prices through support programs, despite price declines in the international market for many key agricultural products.

Prices of Agricultural Inputs

In the United States, the May index of prices paid by farmers for agricultural inputs was 204 (1967=100), the same as in April but 7 percent above May 1976. Livestock feed, seed, fuels, machinery, interest, taxes, and wages have driven farm expenses upward. Feed-livestock price ratios for eggs, broilers, turkeys, and milk all declined from a year ago, but those for pork were slightly stronger.

Japanese farm input prices in January were 6.8 percent higher than in January 1976 (table 3), increasing at a slightly slower rate than prices received by Japanese farmers. While feed prices

were up slightly from a year ago, feeder livestock prices declined 6 percent. Fertilizer prices increased 2.5 percent. Feed-livestock price ratios were more favorable than a year ago for broilers, eggs, and dairy products but were less favorable for hogs.

Canadian price policies held farm input price increases to 4 percent during 1976. Price increases for land, farm labor, machinery, petroleum products, and feed concentrates more than offset declines for fertilizers, seed, grain used in feed, and feeder cattle.

In the EC, input prices continued to rise through the fourth quarter of 1976, particularly for compound feeds for livestock. Indicators from West Germany and the U.K. suggest that the upward price trend continued into the spring of 1977.

Export and Import Prices

As prices of soybeans and soybean products soared, the U.S. export price index began to strengthen after nearly a year of relative stability. The U.S. export price index reached 228 (1967=100) in April, 12 percent higher than a year ago. Soybeans, soybean oil, soybean meal, cotton, tobacco, rice, tallow, cattle hides, and nonfat dried milk were exported at higher prices than a year ago, while export unit values of wheat and corn were 23 percent and 7 percent lower, respectively (table 4).

Among import commodities, the 150-percent increase in coffee import prices (unit values) and the doubling of cocoa bean prices pushed the U.S. import price index up to 332 (1967=100), 70 percent higher than a year ago. Import prices were also higher for beef and veal, rubber, wines, tobacco, bananas, tomatoes, and wool, while sugar was priced a third lower than a year ago.

Japanese and West German agricultural import prices generally moved in the same directions as U.S. import prices. Declining world wheat prices overshadowed slightly increasing beef prices, causing the Canadian index of export unit values to decline.

Despite the general decline in world grain prices, EC users are paying more than a year ago. The May Rotterdam import price for U.S. wheat at $108 a ton was one-third less than a year ago and corn at $111 a ton, was 15 percent less. Nevertheless, because of the EC minimum import price system, EC importers are paying import levies of $127 a ton for wheat and $42 a ton for corn, nearly double the levies of a year ago.

Consumer Food Prices

In the United States, the April Consumer Price Index (CPI) for food was 191 (1967=100), 6.5 percent higher than a year ago. Food prices have been on the upswing since January. Cereals and bakery products, dairy products, fresh fruits and vegetables, eggs, fats and oils, and nonalcoholic beverages have all experienced price hikes at retail. While retail beef is priced at about the same as last year in April, pork is 10 percent lower. Sugar was priced 13 percent lower.

Through the fourth quarter of 1976, U.S. consumer prices for food had remained nearly steady for a year. Bangladesh, Canada, India, Malawi, Paraguay, and Sri Lanka also had steady or declining prices during 1976 (table 5). In contrast, Argentina, Brazil, Chile, Colombia, Ethiopia, Israel, Niger, Peru, Portugal, Italy, Spain, and the United Kingdom experienced increases in food prices of at least 20 percent. (*H Christine Collins: 447-8646*)

U.S. AGRICULTURAL TRADE[2]

U.S. agricultural exports are expected to reach a record $24 billion in fiscal 1977—more than $1 billion or 5 percent above 1975/76. Most of the increase will probably be from higher prices as the volume may show relatively little overall change. However, the U.S. agricultural trade surplus may decline to slightly over $10 billion from the $12¼ billion of a year earlier. A 30-percent gain in the value of agricultural imports is expected in fiscal 1977.

Fiscal 1977 Exports Record High

Export volume of major bulk commodities is expected to be slightly below 1976's 107-million-ton high, but increases are expected for many products, including vegetables, nuts, poultry meat, and animal hides. Higher export prices (unit values) are likely for soybeans, soybean products, cotton, some livestock products, fruits, nuts, and vegetables. The volume of grain exports may be as much as a tenth smaller this fiscal year—reflecting a drop in wheat exports of perhaps one-fourth—and the unit value may be 10 to 15 percent lower. Increased world grain production has increased export competition and reduced import demand in many markets.

The demand for U.S. oilseeds continues very strong this year and U.S. soybean exports have increased to the Soviet Union, Western Europe, and Japan. The world oilmeal supply is very tight, primarily because of reduced U.S. soybean production in 1976 and the small gain this year in Brazilian output. Increased demand for vegetable oil by many developing countries is adding to an already tight situation. U.S. soybean oil exports are likely to total 748,000 tons, nearly 70 percent above a year earlier.

U.S. cotton exports have also rebounded sharply, reflecting lower foreign production, low stocks held by other major exporters, and increased demand stemming from the improved world economic situation. U.S. cotton exports may total about 5.1 million bales, compared with 3.3 million in 1975/76. Other growth commodities during the current year include animal products (especially fats, hides, and skins), fruits, nuts and vegetables.

Substantial increases are expected in U.S. exports to the Middle East, East and Southeast Asia, Japan, Western Europe, and Canada. Exports to the USSR and South Asia are projected well below last year's levels. U.S. agricultural exports to South America are also declining this fiscal year.

Fiscal 1977 Imports Up Nearly One-Third

Fiscal 1977 agricultural imports are expected to climb to around $13.6 billion from $10½ billion in the previous year. Higher prices—especially for coffee, cocoa, tea, and natural rubber—are the main causes. Coffee alone is expected to be up by about $3 billion despite a marginal decline in volume. Volume increases are anticipated for sugar and wines.

Early Prospects for Fiscal 1978

U.S. agricultural exports may decline somewhat in fiscal 1978 if world crop production continues favorable during the balance of the current growing season. Beginning stocks of most commodities except oilseeds and cotton will be much larger than a year earlier. U.S. agricultural exports during fiscal 1978 could reach $27 billion or drop to around $20 billion.

Agricultural imports could total between $12 and $13 billion in fiscal 1978, depending on crop output and the demand situation. (*Dewain H. Rahe: 447-8260*)

[2]This section is based largely on the more detailed review contained in the May 18, 1977 *Outlook for U.S. Agricultural Exports*, published by the Economic Research Service and the Foreign Agricultural Service.

WORLD GRAIN SITUATION LOOSER

1976/77 Situation

Post-harvest reports confirm the marked improvement in the world grain situation forecast earlier in the year. Bumper 1976/77 grain crops have reversed the tight supply conditions of the previous 3 to 4 years. Despite record availabilities, grain consumption has lagged below the trend of the last two decades. This will mean a further buildup in stocks. Carryover at the end of 1976/77 is expected to hit a 6-year high. World grain trade has slowed substantially largely due to improved supply-demand balances in importing countries. Both international prices and the domestic prices of the major trading countries have weakened and are likely to continue well below levels reported a year earlier.

World Production, Consumption, Trade, and Prices

Record area planted and bumper yields pushed the world 1976/77 grain harvest (wheat, milled rice, and coarse grain) up to 1,335 million tons; a crop this large is well above the trend of the last two decades and 7 percent above any previous production record. Consequently, even with carryin stocks low, supplies of grain available for use through the 1976/77 season were in excess of 1,465 million tons—a full 80 million tons above any previous availability (table 6).

While exceptionally large, 1976/77's production increase was concentrated in a few countries—the Soviet Union, the United States, Canada, and a number of the developing countries of Latin America, North Africa, and the Middle East. Harvests in the other countries of the world were largely unchanged or fell below 1975/76 levels as was the case in Europe and Asia. Production increases in 1976/77 were also concentrated in a few grains—particularly wheat, up 18 percent or 64 million tons, and barley up 22 percent or 32 million tons. Only marginal changes were reported in corn, rye, oats, sorghum, and millet. Rice production was reported down 2.5 percent or 5 million tons (tables 7, 8, and 9).

The 1976/77 crop is also less impressive if analyzed in per capita terms. Annual population and income growth generates more than 35 million tons of added grain demand each year. The 113-million-ton increase in production reported for 1976/77 put per capita levels only marginally above 1973/74 levels and put production per capita for the 1970's to date back up to the trend of the 1950's and 1960's.

Despite record availabilities, 1976/77 *grain usage* has increased slowly. While the total for the year will undoubtedly hit a new high, consumption is still likely to fall somewhat below trend for the third consecutive year (tables 6 and 10). Total grain use per capita is reported lagging behind the highs reported from 1972 through 1974 mainly because of feeding. As tables 6 and 10 indicate, lagging growth in consumption has been concentrated in the developed countries with large feed-livestock sectors. Livestock-feed price ratios have improved but are still not favorable enough to generate full recovery. Feed usage is reported up in the Soviet Union and several of the developing countries but not enough to push the world total back up to 1972/73 and 1973/74 highs. Non-feed use of grain continues at or above trend in both the high and low income countries. Total usage in virtually all the developing countries is at or approaching record levels due to this year's good crops, stock drawdowns, or continued high imports.

The supply-demand balances reported to date suggest a 1976/77 world *grain carryover* in excess of 185 million tons, making this year's end stock the largest in 6 years (table 11). While still short of the 17-18 percent target under debate in a number of international organizations, a stock of 185 million tons would be equivalent to about 15 percent of annual global consumption. Stock increases, however, are expected to be concentrated in a few individual countries—the major exporters and the Soviet Union in particular. Increases in wheat stocks are likely to account for four-fifths of the total increase; the coarse grain buildup is likely to be appreciably smaller while rice stocks are likely to decline marginally.

World grain trade in 1976/77 has also slowed somewhat—particularly trade in wheat—reflecting the generally improved supply situation in many of the traditional wheat importing countries. Good grain and non-grain crops cut Soviet imports, while the large carryover accumulated by many developing countries following good 1975/76 crops weakened their import demand. While world imports decreased by 12 million tons or more than 7 percent, export availabilities were up as much as 20 percent or over 30 million tons.

Data to date suggest the United States is absorbing the largest share of the decrease in world exports. More aggressive pricing and marketing policies have improved the Canadian, Australian, and Argentine positions in the world market at the expense of the United States. The U.S. share, however, continues above the lows of the late 1960's and early 1970's.

International prices and the domestic prices of the major trading countries have softened considerably due to the combination of improved supply, lagging demand, dampened import demand, and stock buildup. Wheat prices have fallen and appear to be stabilizing slightly above U.S. loan rates on the U.S. domestic market and, with adjustment for transportation margins, on the world market. Coarse grain prices have not weakened to the same extent as wheat prices due to a relatively tight supply-demand balance in feedstuffs. Wheat and coarse grain prices have moved closer together than their relative feed values would suggest. Rice prices have turned up on a number of domestic markets and on the world market, reflecting the tightening of supplies following a disappointing Asian harvest.

Outlook for 1977/78

Tentative early-season prospects point to slightly smaller 1977/78 world grain crop due to less favorable weather in some areas, and reduced plantings resulting in part from lower grain prices, both in absolute terms and relative to competing crops. Despite some growth in both food and feed usage, grain consumption in 1977/78 is expected to continue to lag below the trend of the last 2 decades for the fourth consecutive year. Projected consumption also may lag behind expected output suggesting a further buildup in stocks. World trade in grains is unlikely to recover to 1972/73-75/76 highs, although some increase from the depressed levels of 1976/77 is forecast. Both international prices and the domestic prices in the major trading countries are forecast to continue near loan rates in the United States and on world markets as well, after adjustment for transportation margins.

World Production, Consumption, Trade and Prices

Reports to date on the 1977/78 world grain crop indicate the harvest is likely to be somewhat smaller than the bumper total reported in 1976/77 (table 6). Information on plantings suggest some reduction in acreage, particularly in the major exporting countries which are facing weakened foreign demand, and real domestic prices approaching pre-1972 lows. Area reductions appear largest in wheat, with marginal adjustments in coarse grains and rice area. More critical than adjustments in area, however, are uncertainties about yields. Weather as of early June indicated growing conditions somewhat less favorable than a year earlier in many key areas.

Weather in the Soviet Union was reported generally good as of June 1, although conditions were somewhat dry in several regions east of the Volga. A crop below last year's record is forecast. Prospects in Western and Eastern Europe are reported above average and well above conditions as of a year ago. Weather and crop conditions were reported less favorable but improving in large winter grain areas of North America. Conditions in spring grain areas are reported improving because of rainfall since early May. Inadequate rainfall has been reported in Asia—particularly in China and India—and parts of Africa—particularly in Algeria, Tunisia, and many of the Sahelian countries.

World grain production (wheat, coarse grains, and milled rice) in 1977/78 is forecast at about 1,320 million metric tons, compared with 1,335 in 1976/77 (table 6). World wheat output is expected to run about 400 million tons and coarse grain, 685 million tons. It is too early to estimate milled rice production, but a crop of around 230 to 235 million tons looks reasonable in view of developments to date. Past variations in yield and area harvested suggest that the final outcome is not likely to vary more than 5 percent in either direction from preliminary estimates in two cases out of three.

The supply-demand balance implied by these production and consumption estimates suggest a second year of large stock buildups, perhaps to a total near 210 to 220 million tons, the equivalent of a little more than 17 percent of annual consumption. Contrary to 1976/77 increases, however, 1977/78 increases are likely to be spread more evenly across wheat and coarse grains; only marginal adjustments are expected in rice stocks. Stock ownership, however, is not likely to become more widely distributed since a large part of the 1977/78 increase would be in the reserves held by the major exporters and the Soviet Union, rather than by the importing countries.

The projected large crops, lagging growth in consumption, and added buildup in stocks are likely to keep prices in the international market and in countries tied to the world market near current 5-year lows. In real terms, wheat and corn prices are likely to slip below the prices reported in the late 1960's and early 1970's. U.S. support prices are likely to shoreup both U.S. and international prices.

Trade is likely to increase only marginally from 1976/77 levels. World 1977/78 grain trade is forecast at about 155 million tons or about 90 percent of record 1975/76 levels. Carryin supplies in major importing countries are large enough to dampen foreign purchases even if the large crop currently forecast should fail to materialize. Competition among the exporters is likely to increase as the year progresses. Supplies available for export by the major traders—including the United States, Canada, Australia, Argentina, Brazil, and Thailand—are estimated in excess of 185 million tons. *(Patrick M. O'Brien: 447-9160)*

After rapid price increases during March and April, recent weeks have brought a significant price decline in the oilseeds complex. Cash prices for U.S. soybeans reached a high of $10.45 per bushel on April 22 but closed at $7.34 on June 21. Oil prices peaked at 32.9 cents per pound on May-26 but closed at 25.5 cents on June 21. Similarly, comparisons for meal were $189 per short ton on June 21 after peaking at $296 on April 22. Regular flows of exports from Brazil are probably responsible for a major part of the market's downturn. Despite present lower prices, the market must be characterized as tight for the remainder of this marketing year. Any sudden change, such as either cancelled orders or new contracts, may have a significant impact on prices.

Review of 1976

Oil and meal supplies were relatively plentiful in calendar 1976 (roughly comparable to the 1975/76 U.S. crop year). Output of oilseeds for 1976 oil production set records as several crops hit new individual production highs on either a global or regional basis. One of these was soybeans, with world production of roughly 67 million tons, compared with 56 million in 1975. Of the 1976 total, the United States accounted for 42.1 million tons, Brazil for 11.2 million tons, and the People's Republic of China (PRC) for 9.5 million tons. Among other countries with greater than expected soybean production was Argentina with 0.7 million tons, compared with 0.5 million tons the previous season. Harvests in the United States and PRC were completed in the fall of 1975, while Brazilian and Argentine harvests were in the the spring of 1976.

1977 World Situation

Vegetable Oils

For calendar 1977 total production of all fats and oils is forecast at 47.8 million tons—well below the 1976 level. For edible vegetable oils, 1977 production is forecast at 31.2 million tons, down 1.6 million tons from 1976. Some production highlights that account for these changes include the 18-percent smaller U.S. soybean crop due to a smaller planted area and reduced yields; the small Canadian rapeseed production of less than 1 million tons, the lowest since 1969; and another poor peanut crop in Nigeria. On the other hand, early in 1977 Brazil harvested another record crop of soybeans, although smaller than expected, and Malaysia is expected to produce and export record quantities of palm oil. Sunflower production in the

Oilmeals

The 1977 situation for oilseed meals is extremely tight and is expected to remain so until the U.S. harvest is well advanced this fall. The December 1976 issue of this publication estimated that world production was down due mainly to the short soybean crop the United States. Since then, the estimate for the Indian peanut crop was revised further downward. However, the principle change affecting world meal supplies is that the Brazilian soybean crop proved to be much smaller than expected in December.

On the demand side, the higher meal prices that have prevailed since last fall have failed to generate the expected rationing effect. Certainly, at least in the United States, a part of the reason is the severe winter which necessitated feeding a higher quality ration.

In addition to its shorter crop, Brazil briefly embargoed exports and made several policy changes that resulted in its exports flowing much more slowly than expected. Because of the already tight situation, these moves brought upward pressure on prices. Recent weeks have seen prices moderate as the flow of soybean exports from Brazil has gained momentum. (*Arthur L. Coffing: 447-9160*)

POLICIES KEY TO MEAT TRADE

Meat exporters face heavy competition as traditional markets remain limited.

The *United States*, the world's largest producer and consumer of meat and, since 1974, leading importer as well, is in the herd liquidation phase of the cattle cycle. Beef production peaked in 1976 at over 12 million tons and is expected to be off some 4 to 6 percent in 1977. Pork output bottomed out in 1975 at just over 5 million tons, recovered by over 7 percent in 1976, and is expected to continue expanding in 1977 sufficiently to offset the anticipated drop in beef production. Thus, combined production of beef and pork is expected to remain near last year's level of just under 18 million tons.

Indicators of U.S. demand continue to point upward—general business activity, industrial production, and consumer income and expenditures. Higher prices are anticipated for beef and cattle along with sustained import demand for beef which, however, will continue to be restrained by the U.S. system of voluntary agreements that affects foreign suppliers.

In the second quarter of 1977, the *European Community* reinstated the variable levy system for beef imports, with its high duties, and tightened restrictions. For the last 3 years, EC net imports of meat have been of the order of 250,000 tons or less, only a fourth of what they were in 1972 and 1973. During this period the EC has used a number of regulatory devices for limiting imports: high variable levies, outright bans on beef imports, and a system of matching imports with exports in varying proportions. Achievement of complete self-sufficiency in beef supplies, together with stable internal prices, has been complicated by developments in production: most importantly, price-depressing effects of herd liquidations related to (1) Europe's pronounced cattle cycle, (2) drought-induced slaughter which was locally severe, and (3) culling of dairy herds which has important beef production implications for Europe's multiproduct farms.

Japan continues to impose quantitative restrictions on beef and veal imports, and the country's 1977 imports of those commodities are expected to fall slightly from the 92,000 tons imported in 1976.

Diversification of *Argentina's* export markets for beef has permitted a recovery of trade volume from the 200,000 to 300,000-ton levels of 1974 and 1975 to a more customary level of twice that in 1976. In those years, markets for Argentine beef shrank throughout Europe and even South America. With production high and exports low, per capita beef consumption, the balancing factor, shot up by 10 kilograms in 1974 and another 10 kilograms in 1975. In 1976 per capita beef consumption reached 88 kilograms, implying that per capita consumption of all meat was over 100 kilograms. The export recovery was aided by increased U.S. demand for cooked beef and timely purchases by the Soviet Union and some Middle Eastern countries. Argentina expects to produce less and export about the same in 1977. *Uruguay* shares some of the same pressures bearing on Argentina.

Production for 1977 is seen continuing to rise in *Mexico* and *Central America*, with a combined beef output of about 1.4 million tons. Exports of about 200,000 tons are expected, with most moving to the United States.

The 1977 combined beef output of *Australia* and *New Zealand* is likely to remain at last year's level of about 2.4 million tons, with a rise in Australia matching a drop in New Zealand. Increased foreign exports this year under the U.S. system of voluntary restraints are more than offset by lowered Canadian quota allotments. The 1977 U.S. allocation for Australia is 296,200 tons product weight and for New Zealand 121,700 tons. It is likely that

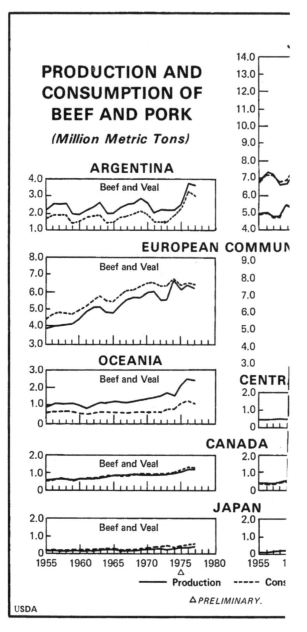

PRODUCTION AND CONSUMPTION OF BEEF AND PORK

(Million Metric Tons)

ARGENTINA
Beef and Veal

EUROPEAN COMMUN

Beef and Veal

OCEANIA
Beef and Veal

CENTR

CANADA
Beef and Veal

JAPAN
Beef and Veal

—— Production ----- Con:

△ *PRELIMINARY.*

USDA

these countries will be promoting sales in other world markets to diversify outlets.

In *Canada*, a 4-percent reduction in 1977 beef production is expected, to 1.1 million tons. Beef exports to the United States are likely to be held to 34,000 tons, just under 1975 levels. Canada's beef imports were 96,000 tons product weight (145,000 tons carcass weight) in 1976. By agreement among the Australian, New Zealand, and U.S. governments, quotas will limit Canada's imports in 1977 to 66,000 tons shared roughly 2:2:1, respectively. Australian and New Zealand quotas are cut by 45 and 23 percent, respectively, compared with Canadian imports from them realized in 1976. (*Donald W. Regier: 447-9160*)

PRODUCTION UP AS POLICIES STIMULATE DAIRY MARKET

Dairy producer price policies and higher yields per cow will continue the increase, projected at 2-percent in 1977, in world milk output. The United States has raised milk support prices 9 percent to $9.00 per hundredweight. In Canada and the European Community (EC), producer target prices have been raised 5 and 3.5 percent respectively. In Canada, where production should equal last year's, the surplus marketing levy has been relaxed. Producer co-responsibility programs have been instituted in the EC where a 1.5-percent levy will become effective September 16.

Price competition with vegetable oils has forced the allowance of subsidies to prevent further increase in butter stocks. Per capita butter consumption in the United Kingdom declined 11 percent in 1976 as domestic prices were being phased into alignment with the EC, while per capita consumption of margerine gained 16 percent. This trend can be expected to continue with Brussels butter retailing in May for $1.86 per pound (U.S. equivalent), more than twice the London price, and margerine at 81 cents per pound. This price difference will have an adverse effect on the UK market for EC butter which absorbed 27 percent of EC consumption and 56 percent of intra-EC butter trade.

Large stocks have caused some countries to greatly subsidize their butter trade. In February, the USSR contracted for 36,000 tons of EC butter, 9 percent of the EC's 1976 yearend stocks, at a price equivalent to 40 U.S. cents per pound, 70 percent less than the intervention price of $1.36. Rumored additional Soviet purchases of the same magnitude led the EC to temporarily extend the time required to approve butter exports. This may have discouraged Soviet expectations of buying at the earlier price, and may have resulted in the Soviet purchase, later this spring, of 3,000 tons of New Zealand butter at an undisclosed price likely to be in line with recent New Zealand-British butter trade at about the equivalent of 75 U.S. cents per pound. A subsequent 6,000-ton Soviet purchase of Australian butter was reported at about 40 cents per pound (U.S. equivalent).

Subsidies have been granted for EC exports of non-fat dry milk (NFDM) to reduce heavy stocks. Prices of EC NFDM for restricted domestic feed uses have varied from the equivalent of 10 to 12.5 U.S. cents per pound this spring, dependent upon a bidding scheme which maintains NFDM's competitive position with soybean meal. This amounts to nearly an 80-percent subsidy. This competitive pricing, inaugurated in early 1977, has succeeded in disposing of 140,000 tons of NFDM, 10 percent of 1976 yearend stocks. New Zealand has sold the Soviet Union 3,500 tons of dry milk, presumably full fat. The indicated price of 40 cents per pound, U.S. equivalent, is well below 80 to 90 cents per pound for which dried whole milk is sold in the United States. (*Howard H. Conley: 447-8646*)

1976/77 WORLD SUGAR OUTPUT A RECORD

Revision of the Soviet sugar output has substantially reduced the 1976/77 world total, now estimated at 86.6 million tons (table 15). This is still a record, about 5 percent above last season and 3.8 million tons in excess of estimated consumption. The world price of sugar (stowed at greater Caribbean ports, including Brazil) averaged about 9 cents per pound in May, some 5 cents less than in May 1976. In mid-June, the price dropped below 8 cents a pound.

World sugarbeet acreage was up 3.3 percent in 1976/77 and beet sugar production, at 33.6 million tons, rose 4.5 percent. The Soviet sugarbeet crop recovered to a record 98.6 million tons (more than 50 percent above 1975/76), but low sugar content and spoilage from poor weather at harvest led to a beet sugar output of only 7.35 million tons (raw value), nearly 2 million less than anticipated.

Cane acreage, mostly in the developing countries, increased 5 percent, and cane sugar produc-

World centrifugal sugar production and consumption
and 1960/61-1976/77 linear trend

	Production		Consumption	
	Actual	Trend	Actual	Trend
	Million metric tons			
1969/70-71/72 ...	71.0	73.9	72.8	71.7
1974/75	78.2	80.1	80.0	80.1
1975/76	82.4	82.2	80.8	82.3
1976/77	86.6	84.3	82.8	84.4
1977/78		86.3		86.5

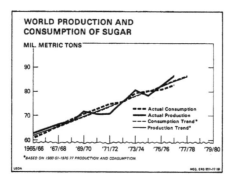

WORLD PRODUCTION AND CONSUMPTION OF SUGAR

tion, about 52.7 million tons, rose 5.8 percent. Cuba's cane crop, just harvested, could be lower than the current estimate of 5.8 million tons, while last year's output is now regarded at upwards of 6.2 million. Thailand's production, growing sevenfold the past decade, is up to 1.8 million tons, of which over 1 million is to be exported. Indonesia's production gains are geared toward a self-sufficiency target of 1.6 million tons by 1982, but record production of 1.25 million tons in 1976/77

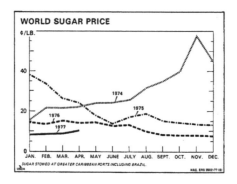

WORLD SUGAR PRICE

of increased domestic needs. The bilateral export contracts of the Philippines total about 2.5 million tons of sugar, but shipments could be delayed to 1978 because of overburdened port facilities.

Negotiations toward a new International Sugar Agreement, held in Geneva in April-May 1977, have been suspended but may be reconvened later this year. (*Robert D. Barry: 447-9160*)

COFFEE SITUATION EASES A LITTLE; COCOA STILL TIGHT

Coffee

The recently completed coffee harvests indicate a 1976/77 world crop of 61.5 million (60 kilogram) bags, somewhat less than earlier anticipated (table-17). World production is 16 percent below the previous harvest and exportable production is down 20 percent. First estimates of the 1977/78 crop point to possibly 70.4 million bags total output and an exportable production of 52.8 million bags, gains of almost 15 and 20 percent, respectively.

About 85 percent of the 1977/78 gain in world production reflects a recovery in Brazil output from

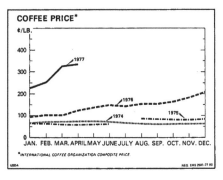

COFFEE PRICE*

*INTERNATIONAL COFFEE ORGANIZATION COMPOSITE PRICE.

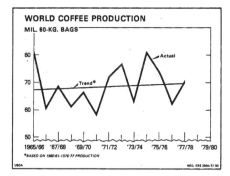

WORLD COFFEE PRODUCTION

*BASED ON 1960/61-1976/77 PRODUCTION

World green coffee production and 1960/61-76/77 linear trend

Year	Actual	Trend	Deviation
	Million 60-kilogram bags		
1969/70-71/72	66.4	68.2	-1.8
1974/75	81.1	69.0	12.1
1975/76	73.6	69.3	4.3
1976/77	[1] 61.5	69.5	-8.0
1977/78	[2] 70.4	69.7	.7

[1] Estimate. [2] Forecast.

the devastating 1975 frost. Brazil's crop, estimated at 17 million bags, would be about 80 percent greater than in 1976/77. At least another season or two beyond 1977/78 will be needed to fully restore Brazil to a more normal coffee harvest of about 25 million bags. Coffee leaf rust in Nicaragua,

detected in November 1976, has infested some 5 percent of the coffee area but will not significantly affect the 1976/77 crop, and the next season's output is expected to still increase perhaps to 975,000 bags or 15 percent.

The May International Coffee Organization composite price for green coffee averaged $2.96 a pound, compared with $1.39 last year and 63 cents in May 1975. Earlier inventory buildups and prospects for a good 1977/78 crop have resulted in a significant downturn in green coffee prices since mid-April. U.S. imports of green coffee beans in 1976 were valued at $2.63 billion or 68 percent above a year earlier, with volume 2½ percent less (table 18).

Cocoa

World cocoa output fell 7 percent to 1.414 million tons in 1976/77 as unfavorable growing conditions reduced African production 13 percent (table 19). World stocks are estimated equivalent to about 3-months' consumption. The New York spot price for "Accra" cocoa beans hit a March 1977 average of $2.06 a pound before easing to $1.89 in April (compared with 88 cents in April 1976). Prices in May, however, turned upward to average $1.96 per pound, reflecting short supplies and reports of dry weather in West Africa. Major relief in world supplies awaits the outcome of the fall harvests. A substantial production boost is foreseen in the

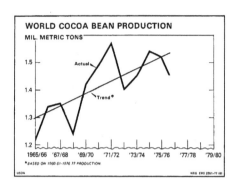

WORLD COCOA BEAN PRODUCTION

World cocoa bean production and
1960/61-76/77 linear trend

Year	Actual	Trend	Deviation
	Million metric tons		
1969/70-1971/72 ..	1.49	1.41	.08
1974/75	1.54	1.50	.04
1975/76	1.52	1.52	—
1976/77	[1]1.41	1.54	-.13
1977/78		1.56	

[1] Estimate.

WORLD COTTON ST

Estimated 1976/77 world cotton consumption of
61 million bales is 2 percent lower than last season
but exceeds production, resulting in a stock drawdown of about 3½ million bales (table 21). When
the 1977/78 season starts on August 1, world
stocks will be around 18.7 million bales, the lowest
since 1953 and equivalent to less than 4 months'
consumption (table 22). An 8- to 10-percent production increase has been predicted for 1977/78, but

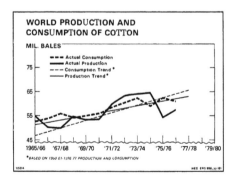

WORLD PRODUCTION AND
CONSUMPTION OF COTTON

use of blends in textile mills. The sharpest absolute cutback has been in the United States. Foreign mill use will likely be down about 2 percent, with notable reductions in India, Pakistan, and Hong Kong. But cotton use is up in South Korea, Thailand, Brazil, and Colombia because of greater domestic textile needs and export demand, and in Turkey and Greece because of sharply rising cotton yarn sales to the EC.

The U.S. export estimate for 1976/77 is 5.1 million (480 lb.) bales, restoring the U.S. position as the world's leading raw cotton exporter (table 23). U.S. stocks will total an estimated 2.7 million bales by August 1, lowest since 1951.

Relatively high cotton prices and plans for stock rebuilding, after 2 years of drawdown totaling 11.5 million bales, have prompted an estimated 6-percent increase in world planted acreage for the 1977/78 season. Prospective world production is estimated at 63 to 64 million bales.

If favorable weather should continue and a yield of 480 pounds per acre is attained, U.S. output could increase some 15 percent to 12.5 to 13 million bales. A rise in cotton output of nearly 2.5 percent is projected for the USSR. A more favorable cotton-wheat price ratio has raised Turkey's cotton acreage about 35 percent. Higher prices and pesticide incentive payments could boost Pakistan's output 40 percent. In Mexico, after 2 years of an official policy favoring food crops over cotton, a 40-percent rise in cotton output is foreseen in reaction

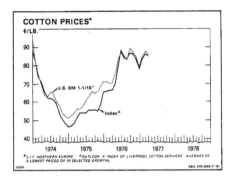

COTTON PRICES*
¢/LB.

*C.I.F. NORTHERN EUROPE △OUTLOOK 'A' INDEX OF LIVERPOOL COTTON SERVICES. AVERAGE OF 5 LOWEST PRICED OF 10 SELECTED GROWTHS.

to attractive cotton prices and shortages of water for wheat and soybeans. High cotton prices should also induce additional cotton acreage in Egypt, Sudan, and India. Continued emphasis on food crops and soybeans may lead to reduced cotton acreages in some countries such as Syria and Brazil.

World cotton consumption in 1977/78, based on the outlook for world economic growth, is forecast to advance less than 2 percent. Nevertheless, the projected world supply-utilization balance is close, and world stocks are likely to expand by less than 2 million bales. (*Robert D. Barry: 447-9160*)

SLOWDOWN IN TOBACCO PRODUCTION

Following moderate growth in 1974 through 1976, world tobacco output is forecast to fall about 2 percent in 1977 (table 24). World consumption in 1977 is expected to increase about 2 percent, the same as last year. Despite higher tobacco leaf prices and cigarette sales taxes in industrial country markets, world output of cigarettes will continue to rise in 1977. The U.S. auction price for flue-cured leaf dropped 5 percent in 1975, but rose 10 percent in 1976, and is expected to rise again in 1977. The U.S. support price for the 1977 crop is up about 7 percent from last year.

The anticipated drop in 1977 world tobacco output of 100,000 tons largely reflects reduced U.S.

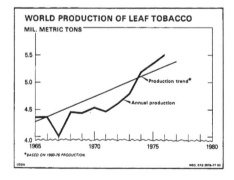

WORLD PRODUCTION OF LEAF TOBACCO
MIL. METRIC TONS

*BASED ON 1960-75 PRODUCTION.

World tobacco production and 1960-75 linear trend

	Actual	Trend	Deviation
	Million metric tons[1]		
1969-71 average ...	4.49	4.73	-0.24
1974	5.18	5.01	0.17
1975	5.32	5.19	0.13
1976	[2]5.50	5.28	0.22
1977		5.37	

[1] Farm-sales weight. [2] Estimate.

tobacco quotas this year. U.S. plantings on 384,000 hectares are 9 percent less, and expected output of 865,000 tons would be roughly 10 percent less than last season. This would be the smallest U.S. crop since 1974. For the world excluding the United States, production in 1977 is forecast at 4.5 million tons, about the same as last year's crop. World flue-cured output would be near 1976's 2.2 million tons, while a marginal rise to 575,000 tons is expected for burley. Oriental tobacco output could fall below the current estimate of 945,000 tons which is about on trend, but somewhat below 1976.

Cigarette production in 1977 is forecast at nearly 4.0 trillion pieces, up just under 2.5 percent. A greater proportion of persons of smoking age and anticipated higher real incomes stimulated a 6.5-percent increase in U.S. output to 693 billion

World cigarette production and 1960-76 linear trend

Calendar year	Actual	Trend	Deviation
	Trillion pieces		
1969-71 average ...	3.17	3.23	-0.06
1974	3.69	3.67	0.02
1975	3.79	3.78	0.01
1976	[1]3.91	3.89	0.02
1977		4.00	

[1] Estimate.

pieces in 1976, but little if any incre₂ in 1977. Outside the United States, ci could rise some 3 percent. Japan, t₂ fifth of U.S. tobacco exports, will ₁ cigarette production after a 6-percent but ample tobacco stocks could imports.

The volume of tobacco exports (de for the world (including Central F could be lower in 1977 because of ₂ demand. U.S. exports may fall below tons, which was the smallest volume ble 25). However, average export uni higher. The U.S. share of world e about a fifth in 1976, compared with 1969-71. Higher U.S. flue-cured and more efficient tobacco use (especiall and increased preferential import qu developing countries have hampered imports are expected to decline some 1977, mainly because of lower tobac cigarettes. Although a smaller vc tobacco exports is anticipated in 197′ is estimated at a record of almost $1. pared with $1.46 billion in 1976. ¹ imports in 1977 are expected near la million. (Charles E. Goode and Rol 447-9160)

REGIONAL AGRICULTURAL DEVELOPMENTS

For a more detailed review of regional agricultural developments in 1976 and 1977, see these reports in the Foreign Agricultural Economic Reports series: *USSR cultural Situation* (FAER-132, April 1977), and reports similarly titled covering *Asic Oceania* (FAER-133, April 1977), *Eastern Europe* (FAER-134, April 1977), *Western E₁* (FAER-135, May 1977), *Western Hemisphere* (FAER-136, May 1977), *People's Repub China* (FAER-137, May 1977), and *Africa and West Asia* (FAER-138, June 1977).

Weather Highlights[3]

In the *United States*, severe cold prevailed in the East and South during January and February, with freezes in the Florida vegetable growing regions in January. Overall, the snowpack was at half the normal or below in the Western States, leading to record-low stream flow predictions. Late April brought widespread above normal precipitation to the Central and Eastern States. Drought conditions persisted in California and in the upper Midwest including the Dakotas, Minnesota, and parts of Iowa and Wisconsin. Rains in the first

[3] A summary of significant conditions since the publication of the last *World Agriculture Situation, WAS-12,* December, 1976. Detailed information on world weather appears the third or fourth week of each month in the *Weekly Weather and Crop Bulletin,* published jointly by the U.S. Departments of Agriculture and Commerce.

half of May eased dry spring conditi da and the northern Great Plains.

The winter months throughout W were generally mild and wet, helpir dry conditions from the previous ye March damaged some crops in so and Spain, while excessive precipitat spring affected crops in Northern It March, dry conditions have persis central plateau and southern coast₂ in other Mediterranean countries experienced less than 50 percent of n during this period.

Most of *Eastern Europe* experienc mal temperatures during the winter r sive precipitation slowed field countries in April and May. Dry we in Bulgaria. *Turkey* received timely resulted in favorable crop conditions.

In the *USSR*, cold snaps during January and February in the Northern Caucasus and lower Volga were possibly damaging to fall-sown crops in areas of light snow cover. January precipitation was below normal but February and March temperatures were above normal for European USSR. An early spring put growth of winter grains and field work 10-20 days ahead of normal schedule, but persistent rains in European USSR hampered spring sowing during the latter half of April. Favorable conditions during the first half of May allowed field work to resume.

Below normal temperatures in the *Peoples' Republic of China* ceased and turned to a period of normal or above normal temperatures from January on. Rainfall during February and March was below normal, with drought conditions in North, East, South, and Central China. Rains began in late March and, with the exception of Kwangtung Province, most areas have received normal to above-normal precipitation since April.

Rainfall has generally been below normal in *India* and *Sri Lanka* with the exception of the rice-growing regions in Southern India and Sri Lanka. While the upper regions of the Brahmaputra, in Assam, experienced severe floods in early June, the monsoon rainfall was deficient during that time in most areas.

Southern and southwestern *Australia* experienced drought-like conditions from January through April, while seasonal tropical activity produced heavy rains in northern Australia in March; most of country received rain in May. A 5-month drought in West Malaysia has been aggravated by the late arrival of the Pacific Monsoon season. Most of *Southeast Asia* is experiencing water shortages due to below normal precipitation.

Normal to above normal rainfall occurred during January through April in parts of *Argentina*, *Brazil,* and *Uruguay*. Drought continued in *Colombia*, but a 2-month drought in *Peru* was broken by January rainfall. Floods were reported on the Andean side of *Bolivia* and Peru in March. Below normal precipitation was experienced in central-south Brazil during February and March. Unseasonably cool temperatures prevailed in Argentina during February, with record lows in Buenos Aires during April. Freezing temperatures occurred over the western Pampa in April and May.

While Morocco experienced normal to above normal rainfall during the winter months, all of northwestern *Africa* has had a very dry spring resulting in serious drought conditions, especially in Algeria and Tunisia. *South Africa* had favorable rainfall conditions throughout these months. The *Sahel* remained seasonally dry through this period. *Western Africa* experienced normal rainfall in the winter months. (*James Dodson: 447-7590*)

United States[4]

U.S. farmers are facing a mixed economic situation. Grain supplies are large, stocks are mounting, and the cost-price squeeze on producers continues. Although livestock product prices have risen, farm prices of cattle and hogs are running below a year ago. Because of low returns to cattle producers, the downtrend in cattle numbers continues and will extend at least well into 1978.

Despite unfavorable conditions for some major groups of commodities, crop and livestock product prices have risen substantially from depressed levels last fall. However, much of the gain reflected tight supplies and strong markets for soybean products and cotton and the impacts of freeze damage on citrus and winter vegetables.

The shortrun outlook for U.S. agriculture has recently been affected by stronger-than-anticipated domestic and foreign demand for U.S. food and fiber supplies. Strong export demand for tight supplies has helped maintain high prices for soybeans, soybean products, and cotton. Domestic demand has rebounded from weather-reduced activity earlier this year.

Many markets, however, are still sensitive to upcoming crop developments. Weather remains the key element.

Farmers have made rapid planting progress, even exceeding last year's unusually fast pace for most crops. Soil moisture supplies have been sufficient in most areas to germinate recent plantings, but crop prospects will be especially dependent on rainfall during the growing season because subsoil moisture is very short in many areas,

If weather remains favorable during the rest of the year, 1977 crop output could match the record levels of the past 2 years. Combined grain and soybean output could exceed last year by around 5 percent, with larger soybean and feed grain crops more than offsetting some drop for wheat and rice.

With large grain crops expected around the world, export demand for U.S. grains would be weaker. A combination of larger supplies, reduced exports, and building stocks could weaken average farm prices for grains and soybeans, although that would likely boost domestic use by the livestock industry.

On the other hand, if weather turned unfavorable both here and abroad, our reduced crop output would be met by strong foreign demand. Grain stocks would be drawn down and prices of most grains and soybeans would average much higher than in 1976/77, except wheat prices which still might average a little lower.

---

[4]This section is based on a more detailed discussion of the U.S. agricultural situation published in *Agricultural Outlook*, AO-22, USDA, June 1977.

Domestic Demand Recovery Goes On

Economic activity in the United States continues rather mixed, although conditions have improved from weather-reduced activity earlier this year. This points to fairly strong demand for food and fiber in coming months.

The economy grew much faster in the first quarter than earlier estimated. Real GNP was up 6.9 percent in January-March following a fourth quarter gain of 2.6 percent. However, much of the added strength was in inventory accumulation. Real final sales actually grew at a slower pace than during the fourth quarter of 1976. Real growth may approach 6.5 percent in April-June before slowing in the second half.

Farm Prices Up Since Late Last Year

Prices received by farmers for all products have risen around 13 percent since last November's low, although they are only about 2 percent above May 1976. However, these gains are primarily centered in the crop area among soybeans, fresh vegetables, and cotton. Moreover, prices of these crops have eased in recent weeks. Grain prices have continued to edge down, with farm prices of wheat down a third from a year ago and corn prices off around 15 percent.

Prices will remain sensitive to crop developments in coming weeks, especially prices of products in tight supply such as soybeans and cotton. If weather continues favorable and large crops are forthcoming, crop prices are likely to decline later this year. On the other hand, very poor weather and reduced crop output would mean strong crop prices during the 1977/78 marketing year.

Although livestock and product farm prices in May were up around 9 percent from last November's lows, they are still some 4 percent below a year ago. However, hog prices have strengthened since mid-May, and cattle prices are now only slightly below a year ago. Prices of livestock and products are likely to be rising seasonally this summer and will probably average a tenth above a year earlier during the second half of this year. Reduced beef output, slackening gains in hog production, and higher dairy supports will help boost prices. (*Robert R. Miller, National Economic Analysis Division: 447-7330*)

Other Developed Countries

Crop Prospects Reasonably Favorable

Crop prospects in the European Community, based on a preliminary report by the EC Statistical Office in mid-May, are generally favorable and overall output is expected to exceed 1976 levels.

Reductions are expected in the area planted to wheat, oats, and sugarbeets while expansions should occur for barley, rye, potatoes, and rapeseed. Due to excessive moisture, seeding of both winter and summer grains has been delayed in much of the EC. The condition of the winter grain crop is considered good, but the condition of summer grains and most other crops is considered less favorable due to damp, cold weather. Although frosts were widespread in France, they are not believed to have caused significant damage to most field crops.

Moisture conditions in parts of southern Europe—Spain, Portugal, and Greece—have not improved nearly as much as in northern Europe since the 1976 summer drought. As a result, crop production may be adversely affected, as is expected for sunflower production in Spain.

Soil moisture in the Prairie provinces of Canada improved significantly with May rain but remains sufficiently low to make crops dependent upon timely rains during the growing season. Spring seeding as of mid-May was nearly completed in Saskatchewan and well advanced in most regions of Manitoba. Progress in Alberta was temporarily delayed by rain and snow when over half of the wheat had been seeded. The Canadian Government has asked producers to cut 1977 wheat plantings some 5 to 6 percent from 1976 levels; production is expected to approximate 18.5 million tons compared with a record 23.5 million tons last year.

Weather conditions in Australia were excellent, except in the west, for the planting of fall crops; some are predicting that area planted to wheat and barley will be a record high. The Government is encouraging an expansion in wheat area. Extremely heavy rainfall in New South Wales in mid-May resulted in some crop losses.

Livestock Prospects Mixed

Beef production in Western Europe is expected to decline in 1977 due to reduced slaughtering. Pork production is expected to increase, but the hog production cycle should peak in the second half of 1977. Egg and poultry meat production should increase moderately. Despite some modification in EC dairy policies (discussed below), milk production will continue to increase this year.

Cattle numbers in Canada dropped 4 percent during 1976, the second consecutive yearly decline. For 1977, cattle slaughter numbers are expected to decline some 5 to 8 percent below last year. Hog numbers increased during 1976 and pork production should rise this year. Broiler production rose sharply in 1976 and should continue to increase slightly in 1977. Output of turkeys, produced under quotas, should increase about 3 percent. January-April milk production has declined slightly from

1976 but for the remainder of the year should be close to last year's.

Australia and New Zealand are expected to show somewhat diverse livestock production patterns in 1977. Australia will cut milk and wool production, while meat output may increase slightly; New Zealand is expected to increase milk, wool, mutton, and lamb production, while cutting beef production.

Japanese farmers should experience continued profitability in livestock production in 1977. Further production increases are expected for beef, pork, poultry meat, eggs, and milk. Meat import policies are manipulated to affect producer prices. For example, a duty waiver on pork has been suspended in order to strengthen domestic prices, and the beef import quota for October 1976-March 1977 was 40,000 metric tons compared with 45,000 metric tons in the previous 6-month period.

Recent Policy Actions

The EC reached a final decision on 1977/78 farm prices and related programs on April 25-26, 1977. Farm prices will increase on average nearly 4 percent[5], slightly above EC Commission proposals and substantially below increases (expressed in units of account) in prior years. The target price for all soft wheat was increased by 4 percent. Soft wheat is classified as either feed wheat or as quality (bread) wheat with feed wheat support prices set nearly 12 percent below the reference price for quality wheat. The objective is to make soft wheat, for which the EC is a surplus producer, more competitive with feed grain. Barley support prices were also increased 3.5 percent to match the 120.06 units of account set for feed wheat; corn support prices were increased 5.2 percent and are now less than 2 percent below the support prices of wheat and barley. The EC's goal is a single support price for all feed grains.

Despite substantial stockpiles of nonfat dry milk (NFDM) and butter in the EC, the support prices of these commodities were increased approximately 3 percent. All member states can grant consumer subsidies for butter with special provisions being made for the United Kingdom. The EC Council adopted plans for structural rationalization of the dairy sector which include: additional measures to

---

[5]On the basis of units of account set by the EC Council. Actual price changes will vary substantially by country due to monetary adjustments. For detailed information on the EC decisions, see these Economic Research Service publications: *Western Europe Agricultural Situation—Review of 1976 and Outlook for 1977.* FAER No. 135, May 1977 and *European Community's 1977/78 Farm Prices and Related Policy Actions,* Supplement to FAER No. 135, June 1977.

boost butter consumption, the imposition (effective September 16) of a producer co-responsibility levy of 1.5 percent on the value of most milk sales, the granting of premiums for nonmarketing of milk and the conversion of dairy herds to beef herds, the discontinuation of financial aid for purchasing dairy cows, the provision of payments to eliminate animals with specified diseases, the financing of school-milk programs, and the provision of aid for investments necessary to increase the amount of liquid skim milk fed to hogs. The EC is continuing the sale of NFDM for pig and poultry feed by announcing tenders and making "fixed price" sales.

Support price increases were approved by the EC Council for numerous other commodities including durum wheat, rice, rapeseed, sugar, cattle, and hogs.

Canada and Poland signed a new 3-year grain accord in April, doubling the quantities of Canadian grain destined for Poland between January 1, 1977 and January 1, 1980. The agreement, negotiated by the Canadian Wheat Board and Rolimpex (the Polish grain trading agency), includes between 1.5 to 2.4 million tons of wheat, barley and oats. In late May, the Canadian Wheat Board announced the sale of 3 million tons of wheat to the People's Republic of China for delivery between August 1977 and July 1978.

Canadians are debating the establishment of a broiler marketing agency similar to the Canadian Turkey Marketing Board. Approval of such an agency could have a detrimental impact on U.S. broiler exports to Canada. The quota on turkeys and turkey meat imports was 1,800 tons in 1976, but an additional 3,800 tons (mostly large turkeys) were imported under supplementary licenses for the institutional trade.

The United States and Canada have agreed to limit their beef trade in 1977. Canadian beef exports to the United States will be limited by their voluntary agreement to 34,000 tons, while U.S. beef exports will be limited to 11,000 tons as part of a global quota imposed by Canada.

A recent report by the Canadian Tariff Board recommends increased seasonal protection for Canadian commercial growers of fresh fruits and vegetables and safeguards against distress-priced imports. Also recommended is the removal of all off-season duties on fresh fruits and vegetables since these duties provide little benefit to Canadian growers and result in higher consumer prices. The United States is Canada's major supplier of fresh fruits and vegetables.

The April 12 decision by the U.S. Customs Court imposing countervailing duties on subsidized electronic exports from Japan to the United States could have significant indirect implications for

U.S. agriculture. If the decision is upheld in the appeals court, if similar decisions are taken against other commodities, and if additional legal initiatives now underway are consummated, these collective actions might ultimately have an unfavorable impact on U.S. agricultural exports. Japan is also under pressure from the EC to import more commodities from the Community and reduce the heavy trade surplus with the region.

Ortho-phenyl-phenol (OPP), which is highly effective in preventing spoilage of citrus fruit during shipment, was recently added to a list of acceptable food additives (within specified limits) by Japan. The ban has been a major factor limiting the export of U.S. fruit to Japan. However, recent reports indicate that consumer groups in Japan are organizing to boycott all OPP-treated citrus fruit.

Japan may soon raise the resale (wholesale) prices of wheat and rice 15 and 8 percent, respectively. The resale price of wheat was increased 20 percent in February 1976 and 16.5 percent in July 1976, compared with a price increase of only 10.2 percent for rice in September 1976. A continuing Government policy of raising the wheat resale price at a faster rate than the rice resale price will have a dampening effect on the consumption of wheat products.

U.S. Agricultural Exports

U.S. agricultural exports to Western Europe are forecast at $8.3 billion in fiscal 1977. This is nearly 35 percent of total expected U.S. exports, and $1 billion higher than a year earlier, with the increase going largely to EC member countries. Japan will remain the single largest market for U.S. agricultural exports, with a forecast $3.6 billion—up $400 million from 1975/76. The Canadian market for U.S. agricultural exports is forecast at $1.6 billion, up more than a tenth from a year earlier. (*Reed E. Friend: 447-6809*)

USSR

Spring arrived somewhat early, with warmer than normal temperatures in European USSR during February, March, and early April. Precipitation during this period generally ranged from near normal to significantly above normal. Growth of crops in the southern part of the country started 10 to 20 days earlier than usual, and spring field work got off to a good start.

Weather during most of April, however, was very rainy and quite cool in European USSR. This interfered with spring field work and slowed crop growth, but warm, dry weather during the first several weeks of May in European USSR permitted a very sharp rebound in the tempo of field work. Weather in Asiatic USSR was very favorable for conducting spring field work but resulted in a rather rapid decrease in soil moisture during the past several months.

Soil moisture in areas west of the Volga region ranged from slightly above to well above normal by June 10, but the southern half of the Urals region and the upper two-thirds of the Volga region, and Asiatic USSR were appreciably drier.

The area planted to spring crops through mid-April was about equal to the average planted by that date in 1972-76. As of April 25, however, there was a lag of 8 million hectares or about 3 days at the average seeding rate. Grain seeding was somewhat delayed, but the most serious delay was in sunflower and corn planting. The lag in spring seeding was made up during the first half of May. Sunflowerseed planting on collective and state farms was completed about on schedule on 4.5 million hectares, although a fairly large portion of the crop was sown somewhat later than normal. Cotton was planted on 2.97 million hectares, with the work being completed by May 16, a little earlier than usual. Sugarbeet planting was also essentially completed by this date on an area of over 3.7 million hectares. Potatoes generally were planted ahead of last year's delayed schedule, and vegetable planting continued ahead of schedule into early June. Spring planting was reported to be completed successfully on June 14 with 151 million hectares planted to all spring crops.

Favorable conditions and larger supplies of feed for Soviet livestock this year were reflected in increased livestock numbers on state and collective farms during the first 4 months of 1977. As of May 1, total cattle were up 3 percent, cow numbers up 4 percent, and sheep and goats up 3 percent from a year earlier. The largest gains were made in poultry and hog numbers, which were up 19 and 15 percent, respectively, above the depressed year-earlier levels. Growth in total inventories of cattle, cows, and especially hogs was faster during January-April than in the same period of the preceding 4 years. Poultry inventories continued to expand but at a slower-than-average rate. Growth in sheep and goat inventories also showed above-average gains. Good increases in livestock inventories can be expected during 1977 if current favorable conditions continue. Hog numbers may be rebuilt this year to the record January 1975 level.

Soviet industrial output of meat during January-May 1977 was 4 percent larger than a year earlier owing to strong recovery in April and May; whole milk products increased 3 percent and butter rose 25 percent. (*Angel O. Byrne: 447-8380*)

Eastern Europe[6]

Prospects for the harvest of small grains are good. Winter grains developed very well. Fall sowing was completed in optimal time, except in the southern countries where wheat followed late harvested corn. Planned wheat sowing was 65,000 hectares short in Yugoslavia. Winterkill throughout Eastern Europe was minimal. Springlike weather early in February allowed resumption of field work. A cool and frosty April retarded growth somewhat, but recovery was quick in May. Frost damage to peaches, apricots, and grapes was reported in the German Democratic Republic (GDR), Hungary, and Yugoslavia. Precipitation and soil moisture were above average during the spring, except for Bulgaria where dryness prevailed.

Based on fall sown area and spring sowing plans, grain area will be larger than in 1976 by 500,000 hectares (ha.). Poland accounts for most of the increase. In Poland, corn for grain—insignificant just a few years ago—will be sown on 110,000 ha., doubling the 1976 area.

An expansion of 80,000 ha. in oilseed planting—primarily to sunflowerseeds in Yugoslavia and soybeans in Romania—is anticipated. The harvested area of rapeseed will increase slightly in Poland due to below average winterkill. Plans call for a 50,000-ha. expansion of sugarbeets in Poland. Most area increases will occur as a result of a reduction in area devoted to forage crops and fallow land.

As a consequence of last year's drought, grain imports by the northern countries were above normal during 1976/77. If the good harvest prospects are realized, grain imports can be reduced in 1977/78. Regardless of the harvest results, these countries will depend on imported grain to varying degrees during this decade. In addition to the Polish and GDR understandings with the United States, Poland has an agreement to import 1.5 to 2.4 million tons of Canadian grain during 1977-79. The Soviet Union apparently is under no specific obligation to export grains to Eastern Europe.

The southern countries are expected to be net grain exporters in 1977/78. Hungary will export about half a million tons of grain to the USSR and a total of 1 million tons to Czechoslovakia, GDR, and Poland under long-term agreements. Romania and Yugoslavia likely will increase stocks or exports.

Imports of oilseed products are expected to continue approximately at the level of the past few years. Soybean and soybean product imports are estimated to be in the range of 1.3 to 1.5 million tons unless an unfavorable soybean-corn price

<hr>

[6]Northern countries: Czechoslovakia, German Democratic Republic (GDR), and Poland; Southern countries: Bulgaria, Hungary, Romania, and Yugoslavia.

ratio causes a shift from protein feed to more grain imports.

Domestic marketings of red meat were down from last year's level in the northern countries during the first quarter of 1977. Chances are good for increased output in the livestock sector if harvest prospects are realized. Some setback was reported in Romania where the March 4 earthquake destroyed or damaged several hundred barns. In contrast, Hungary reported a sizable increase in meat output. Stepped-up imports of meat offer the shortrun solution to satisfaction of domestic demand in the northern countries; revitalization of the livestock sector with adequate imports of concentrated feed is the longer term solution.

The meat self-sufficiency ratio has deteriorated in the northern countries. As a result of a 23-percent decline in hog numbers during 1976, Poland became a net meat importer. Poland apparently will continue as a net importer in 1977 with imports of about 100,000 tons. In contrast, Hungary resumed hog exports in the first quarter of 1977 and increased exports of slaughter sheep and poultry, and eggs by 19, 29, and 21 percent, respectively, compared with the same period of 1976. Exports of slaughter cattle, however, declined 26 percent owing to a stock rebuilding policy. (*Thomas A. Vankai: 447-8380*)

People's Republic of China

Last year was disappointing for agriculture in the People's Republic of China (PRC). Weather problems were the primary cause of an estimated 3-million-ton decline in grain production to 267 million tons. Although wheat production rose during the year, rice and miscellaneous grain production was down. Soybean production was off, as was production of other oilseeds, with the exception of peanuts. This has contributed to a sharp drop in soybean exports and a very tight edible oil situation.

Prospects for PRC agriculture in 1977 appear uncertain. Unfavorable weather during winter and early spring has threatened winter crops. In addition, China also faces the more basic question of the future direction of its politics and economy—and consequently agriculture.

Below normal temperatures occurred in all of China in November and December 1976. But from January 1977 on, temperatures turned normal. The most serious problem facing Chinese agriculture this year has been below normal precipitation in most growing regions. By March, the State Council and provinces were calling for an all-out effort to fight "the most serious drought" since 1949.

The most critically affected areas were in North, East, and Central China, where winter wheat and other winter crops were emerging from dormancy earlier than usual due to the early onset of warm weather, as well as in the early rice areas in the South, notably in southern Kwangtung Province.

Since mid-March weather patterns have progressively improved. Light rain fell in late March in parts of the critical areas, and in April normal to above-normal precipitation occurred in more than 70 percent of crop-producing provinces, virtually eliminating drought conditions in Central China and the lower third of the North China Plain. In May, above normal rain fell in almost all major agricultural areas.

As a result of improved rainfall and the massive mobilization of the rural labor force, the drought has eased considerably. On May 9 the New China News Agency reported that the drought had been overcome, that virtually all early rice had been transplanted on a greater acreage than last year in the southern provinces including Kwangtung, and that sowing of spring sown crops was about completed.

Although the weather has improved, the drought has taken its toll of winter crops, particularly in the nonirrigated areas. By now the harvest of winter sown crops is about complete. Because of the dry spring, it is probable that most of the early harvested crops will be somewhat below last year's records. However, the prospects for early rice are better than in 1976 because of more favorable weather and expanded area.

Moreover soil moisture reserves remain low, especially in North China. Timely rainfall will be very important for the remainder of the year for spring sown crops in the North and the rice crop in South China.

China's political and economic conditions are likely more favorable for agriculture this year compared with the disruptions of 1976. With the new leadership striving for stability, unity, and economic growth, 1977 production activities are expected to be more concerted to reach greater output in all economic sectors.

After maintaining a low profile through much of 1976, China has increased its agricultural trade dramatically in recent months. Grain purchases have jumped sharply from the 2.1-million-ton low import level of 1976. With the recent purchase of 3 million tons of Canadian wheat, China's purchases of grains (all wheat), since November 1976 now total about 8.5 million tons. Based on contracts signed to date, calendar 1977 grain imports will be at or above 6.5 million tons. This will be a record level of wheat imports, but total grain imports will be below the record 7.6 million tons imported in calendar 1973. About 6 million tons are already scheduled for delivery during the 1977/78 marketing year. This figure is expected to rise because some additional purchases seem likely later this year for delivery during the first half of 1978.

In part, higher grain imports reflect an anticipated reduction in the early 1977 harvest and uncertainty about the late harvest caused by dry weather in North China. But a low level of beginning stocks caused by low imports in 1975 and 1976 and an apparent failure to meet the 1976 state procurement plan appear to be important factors. Despite the large increase in imports, there is no clear indication of a basic long-run change in China's grain purchasing behavior.

China's rice exports in 1977 will apparently be below the estimated 1 million tons exported in calendar 1976, despite favorable world rice prices and market opportunities. This most likely results from stagnant rice production in recent years and a probable tight stock situation. As a result, China's net imports of grain during calendar 1977 will be a record, about 6 million tons.

Soybean exports in calendar 1977 are expected to remain at low levels (below 200,000 tons), and imports of 378,000 tons of soybeans have been contracted for the year, making China a net importer of soybeans for the first time since 1974 and only for the second time since 1949.

The U.S. share of the increase in agricultural trade has been small. Prospects for substantial additional U.S. sales in 1977 appear limited at this time. (*Charles Y. Liu and Frederic M. Surls: 447-8380*)

Asia

Weather conditions varied widely throughout Asia, and countries experienced both favorable and unfavorable changes in their agricultural situation from earlier estimates. *India's* agricultural production in 1976/77 (July-June) will be down considerably because of reduced output of some major crops—21 percent for peanuts, 12 percent for rice, and 5 percent for wheat. Total food grain production, estimated at 110 million tons, will be down from last year's record 120.8 million tons. Erratic monsoon rainfall in 1976 caused rice output to decline from 49.5 million tons in 1975/76 to about 43.5 million tons this season. Despite a winter drought, good performance of high-yielding wheat varieties allowed Indian farmers to harvest about 27 million tons of wheat this year—down from 28.3 million tons in 1976. Rainfall so far in 1977 has been far below normal in most of India, although floods ravaged Assam in June. Production of tea, tobacco, and jute increased in 1976/77, contributing to the strong showing in agricultural exports.

India's total agricultural exports are expected to reach $1.7 billion in 1977 because of higher prices for tea, coffee, tobacco, and some less important items. Sugar exports this year will be about half the 846,000 tons exported in 1976 because of a policy to keep more sugar for domestic use. Further exports of peanuts are banned and exports of onions, cotton, and vegetable oils are restricted.

India's agricultural imports are expected to remain above $1 billion in 1977 but down from last year's $1.4 billion, mostly because of the sharp reduction in wheat imports. Sharp hikes in imports of soybean oil, peanut oil, and cotton this year will offset some of the dramatic reduction in wheat imports. Plans to export wheat to the Soviet Union or other markets to relieve storage problems have been reported. Government grain stocks exceed 19 million tons, but losses due to pests are high.

Pakistan's wheat harvest is now estimated at about the same level as last year's 8.4 million tons, a less optimistic figure than the January official Pakistani estimate of over 8.8 million tons. Unusually warm weather in late February and early March increased shriveling of wheat grain, and late rains at harvest time adversely affected wheat yields.

With the smaller harvest, Pakistan now expects to import 600,000 to 800,000 tons of wheat, about double the previous estimate based on the earlier production forecast. Most of the wheat imports will likely come from the United States under P.L. 480 and CCC (Commodity Credit Corporation) loans.

Because of a second consecutive low cotton crop in 1976, availability of domestic cottonseed oil has decreased considerably, thus increasing imports of soybean and palm oil. Pakistan expects to import about 300,000 tons of vegetable oil during 1977, with the bulk of soybean and cottonseed oil coming from the United States under P.L. 480 and CCC loans. Pakistan may also import palm oil from Malaysia and Indonesia, and some soybean oil from Brazil.

After 3 years of severe drought, *Sri Lanka* harvested a bumper major season rice crop of about 750,000 tons in 1977, compared with 580,000 tons last year. This has reduced the Government's rice import requirements from 450,000 tons in 1976 to about 300,000 tons in 1977.

The food grain situation in *Bangladesh* is somewhat uncertain. While some local areas suffered severe flood damage, the country has experienced no major weather catastrophe so far this year. The Bangladesh Government, viewing food grain commitments from donor countries as inadequate, reentered the commercial food grain market with wheat purchases of 50,000 tons from Australia and rice purchases of 60,000 tons from Thailand and 40,000 tons from Burma. Some observers, however, viewed these purchases as unnecessary since stocks were considered adequate and negotiations were underway to increase P.L. 480 shipments by 150,000 tons.

Thai rice exports for 1977 are now forecast to reach at least 1.6 million tons, slightly higher than previous estimates. This estimate is based on January through mid-May exports in excess of 1 million tons and additional commitments for 600,000 tons. Fulfilling export commitments for the final 600,000 tons, however, may require stocks to be reduced sufficiently to cause upward pressure on domestic rice prices. However, this upward pressure may be partially offset by the recent curtailment of illicit border trade, making some 150,000 to 200,000 tons of rice available for domestic consumption or legal exports. Should the domestic price of rice increase, the Thai government may request exporters and importers to delay some shipments until after the November harvest begins.

Planting of early corn for 1977/78 has now begun in major growing areas. Increased domestic and foreign demand for Thai corn has encouraged farmers to expand 1977/78 acreage, with production forecast at 3.5 million tons and exports at 2.5 million tons.

Severe cold weather caused *South Korea's* 1977 barley harvest to fall about 30 percent below the 1.8 million tons produced in 1976. A combination of buoyant demand, improved foreign exchange reserves, and the small barley crop might cause South Korea's grain imports to reach 4 million tons in 1977, including over 2 million tons of wheat, 1.5 million tons of corn, 400,000 tons of barley, and 100,000 tons of rice.

Indonesia's main season rice harvest (April-June) is reportedly much improved, enabling the total 1977 output to be in the 16-million-ton range, significantly above the harvest of the past 3 years. The increased output should prevent rice imports from rising above last year's level of about 1.4 million tons. Thailand and the United States will again be Indonesia's major rice suppliers, with most of the remainder coming from other Asian countries.

The problem of overabundance of sugar that plagued the *Philippines* in late 1976 and early 1977 and resulted in delayed harvesting has been partially solved. While huge sugar sales to the USSR and the PRC have been contracted, questions have been raised as to whether the Philippines can move the volume of sugar involved.

Malaysia's monsoon rainfall was far below normal during early 1977, causing severe drought and delayed rice planting in the important Muda rice-growing region. As a result, rice output during the current year will be reduced by at least 90,000 tons. Officials are already planning for a sharply lower 1978 rice crop, and rice imports may reach 230,000 tons or more during 1977.

U.S. agricultural exports to *Hong Kong* are likely to reach $309 million in 1977 as the value of poultry, ginseng, and horticultural product shipments increase and cotton shipments triple. (*Asia Program Area: 447-8106*)

Latin America

Last year's drought reduced agricultural prospects for 1977 in some Caribbean areas; adverse weather is expected to restrict production in Brazil and in the North Andean highlands, but heavy rains provided excellent conditions in other Latin American areas. A recovery is anticipated for coffee and cotton, and sugar output may rise above the 1976 record. Oilseed production will continue to increase and record harvests of feedgrains are in prospect. In contrast, a sharp decline is anticipated for rice, wheat production may fall below the 1976 record, and expansion of beef output will probably be limited.

Exports of coffee, sugar, bananas, grains, and livestock products continued rising. Imports of grains and other food commodities reflected larger domestic supplies and serious economic problems in some countries. U.S. agricultural imports from Latin America for January-March 1977 were valued at $1.5 billion, up sharply from the first-quarter 1976 record of $1 billion. U.S. agricultural exports for January-April fell from $703 million in 1976 to $581 million this year.

Argentina expanded the area of the current 1977 harvests, particularly sorghum, cotton and soybeans. A sharp recovery is forecast for corn (8.5 million tons), and a record sorghum harvest (6.7 million tons) added to unusually large wheat supplies. Expanded cottonseed, flaxseed, peanuts, and a record soybean harvest is expected to increase total oilseed production by nearly 20 percent.

Most of the 6 million tons of exportable wheat from the large 1976 crop was committed by February this year. Grain exports were facilitated by improved administration and the opening of a new deepwater channel at Rosario on the Parana river. Record 1977 grain shipments, estimated at about 13.5 million tons, will be supplemented by expansion in oilseeds and oilseed products, cotton and sugar. Livestock products should also help raise export earnings.

Brazil's planted area for early 1977 harvests continued to increase, and growing conditions were unusually favorable in late 1976. However, the citrus and peanut crops were damaged by excessive January rains, and some crop yields were reduced by hot, dry weather through February and early March. Expanded area is expected to increase the current corn harvest above the 17.9-million-ton record of 1976. A strong recovery is anticipated for coffee, from 570,000 tons in 1976 to about 1 million this year. Cotton production is estimated significantly above the low 1976 outturn in spite of drought damage. However, current estimates of the

soybean harvest have been revised downward from earlier forecasts of 12.6 million tons. Rice plantings were cut back and drought reduced yields. Production problems of the past 2 years are expected to discourage expansion in wheat and the October-November harvest is forecast near the record 3.1 million tons for 1976.

Brazil's agricultural exports for January-March of $1.6 billion were nearly double the year earlier value. Brazil forecasts 1977 exports at $9 billion, up 50 percent from the record last year. Larger shipments and higher prices pushed January-March coffee earnings above $1 billion, nearly four times those of January-March 1976. Volumes for sugar, corn, rice, and meats were larger, but soybeans and soybean products were lower because of a temporary March suspension of sales and the imposition of a contribution quota or tax. The tax was initially set at 7 percent and raised to 12 percent late in April. However, exports of soybeans and products are expected to be near the record high 1976 volumes and, with higher prices, should add to earnings. In contrast, agricultural imports will fall sharply due mainly to the large 1976 wheat harvest.

Mexico's wheat area for 1977 was cut back because of government expropriations of irrigated lands in the north-Pacific state of Sonora. Rust damage resulted in some abandonment, and the April-June harvest is estimated down sharply from the record 3.1 million tons in 1976. Cotton plantings increased through the northern irrigated areas, and production is estimated to be 40 percent above the low 1976 outturn. Shortages of irrigation water persist in some north-Pacific zones, but supplies were replenished and moisture conditions remain favorable for pasture and planting of later crops in most other areas. Mexico anticipates a further expansion in corn, which reached a record 9.6 million tons in 1976. Some recovery in soybeans and safflowerseed is expected, and later harvests of sorghum, rice, and beans may reach record highs this year.

Mexico's shift from self-sufficiency in wheat to a significant deficit and the need to offset shortfalls in 1976 oilseed and oilseed products output will make agricultural imports larger in 1977. However, a further decline is anticipated for purchases of feed grains. The current coffee harvest is estimated below 1976 and domestic shortages led to imposition of an April 1 domestic quota of one 60-kilogram bag for each two bags exported. Other commodity exports expanded, including fruits and vegetables, cattle, and meat. U.S. agricultural imports from Mexico for January-March rose sharply from $194 million in 1976 to $334 million in 1977, but U.S. agricultural exports for the period fell from $106 million to $86 million due partly to increased competition from Argentina and Brazil in the Mexican market for feed grains and soybeans.

Drought in *Central America* was followed by heavy rains which reduced yields of some late 1976 coffee crops but improved pastures and prospects for early 1977 harvests, including those for cotton and sugarcane. Unusually dry conditions in the Caribbean were also relieved by the early onset of the 1977 rainy season; in Cuba, intermittent, heavy rains caused flooding and hampered the recent sugar harvest. However, drought persisted in north-Andean Highlands, and a 10-percent reduction is forecast for early food crops in Colombia. Pastures and food crops in the Peruvian highlands were seriously damaged by frosts and floods following the 1976 drought. In contrast, a sharp recovery is estimated for recent harvests of grains in Chile. In spite of record December-February precipitation, Uruguay's feed grain and rice crops are expected to be larger this year, but a smaller cattle herd may restrict beef production. (*Howard L. Hall: 447-8133*)

Africa and West Asia

North Africa

Dry weather this spring has sharply reduced wheat and barley crops in *Algeria, Morocco, and Tunisia*. These three countries will probably have to import more than 3 million metric tons of wheat to make up the deficit; imports in 1976 were about 2 million tons.

Total grain production in Morocco is estimated at 3.1 million tons, far below the 4.5 million considered normal. Production in Algeria may be 30 percent below normal, and Tunisia's total grain output will not exceed 850,000 tons compared with 1,150,000 last year. (Herbert H. Steiner: 447-8966)

Egypt's total agricultural imports might reach $2 billion in 1977—up from $1.6 billion in 1976—and the U.S. share might reach 40 percent compared with 28 percent in 1976. The U.S. Agency for International Development (AID) announced the approval of $175 million for commodity loans including funds for 152,000 tons of corn, 20,000 tons of cottonseed oil, 20,000 tons of poultry, and 5,000 tons of butter.

In addition to the AID loan, Egypt has already been allocated PL 480 financing for 1.5 million tons of wheat and flour, 500,000 tons of corn, 5,000 tons of tobacco, and 4,000 tons of dry beans. (*John B. Parker, Jr.: 447-8107*)

East Africa

The East African Community (EAC) of Kenya, Tanzania, and Uganda has had agreements on tra-

ding as well as on the operation of common services such as railroads and telecommunications.

In recent years, relations among these countries have deteriorated, and the cooperation needed to make the EAC work well has been lost. The immediate interests of each country now seems to take precedence. As Tanzania moves toward socialism, the remaining ties between Kenya and Tanzania seem to be breaking up. Tanzania recently closed its border with Kenya. Concern over the distribution of the benefits from the common services has caused the breakdown of these services.

Tanzania and Uganda reject the role of being raw material suppliers to Kenya. As one result, U.S. cotton could replace Tanzanian cotton exports to Kenya.

Uganda's agriculture is being harmed by the breakdown in the Community. Its coffee exports to Kenya's Mombasa port have been delayed for one reason or another. The Government has tried to interest buyers to come to Uganda and make their own transport arrangements for the coffee. Since May, Uganda has turned to the costly method of air freighting coffee to Djibouti.

There is some hope that cooperation in scientific research including agricultural research will continue as an E.A.C. endeavor. An example of this would be the continuation of the excellent U.S.-assisted corn breeding program. Possibilities for greater cooperation in seed production and distribution among these countries still exist. (*Lawrence A. Witucki: 447-8966*)

French Territory of Afars and Issas. Independence was not opposed by the French when on May 8, 1977, the people of the French Territory of Afars and Issas voted for independence after 93 years of French rule. Independence is set for June 27, 1977. The Territory's city of Djibouti is a major deep water port and of great importance to Ethiopia for trade reasons. Djibouti, by virtue of a rail link with Ethiopia's Addis Ababa, is Ethiopia's most important trade depot. Both Ethiopia and Somalia see it as a natural part of their territories.

Ethiopia's coffee exports are lagging this year, as trade sources report that only about 32,000 tons had been exported by May 15 compared with a normal 45,000 tons. This reduction in exports is not a consequence of Government policy, but rather the result of the Coffee Exporters Association's urging that the export surtax be based on a different reference price than Santos IV. The *Sudan* cotton crop harvested in 1976/77 was well below the average production, but early sales of cotton indicate that 1977 earnings will be surprisingly good. The Cotton Public Corporation reports sales increases of 228,000 bales over the sales in the spring of 1976. Influenced by the firm demand for cotton, Sudan has now reversed its long-term policy of gradually reducing the area devoted to long staple cotton and the area will be instead slightly increased. Also, short and medium staple area will be increased by some 100,000 feddans (103,800 acres), three-quarters of which will come with the opening of phase 1 of the new Rahad scheme this summer. (*H. Charles Treakle: 447-8966*)

South Africa

The outlook for this year's grain production in South Africa continues favorable. Corn production is forecast at 9.6 million metric tons. Although the area planted is the lowest since the drought of 1973, relatively high yields of about 34 bushels per acre are expected. Export availability during the current marketing year is expected to be about 3 million tons. During the past year, corn exports were about 1.5 million tons.

Wheat deliveries to the Wheat Board this year are expected to be a record high of about 2.3 million tons. Wheat is in surplus, with the current producer price of about $3.83 a bushel, considerably above recent world market prices. (*Lawrence A. Witucki: 447-8966*)

West Asia

The 1977 Turkish wheat crop is estimated at 13.5 million tons, 3.9 percent above last year's record crop. This is the third consecutive excellent crop and Turkey has huge stocks on hand. Turkey did not sell any wheat in 1976. In 1977, 700,000 tons have already been sold and an additional equal amount is likely to be sold before the end of the summer.

During the 1977/78 marketing year, Turkey will have approximately 2 million tons of wheat for export. However, the actual shipments will likely be limited to 1 million tons, because of limited port and transportation capacities.

The *Iranian* grain situation looks good; recent rains have been favorable. Grain yields are expected about the same as last year, with 5.5 million tons of wheat, 1.1 million tons of barley, and 850,000 tons of rice. Imports of wheat for the 1977/78 year are expected near 1 million tons, most from the United States. Feed grain imports are estimated at 800,000 tons, with about half likely to come from the U.S. Rice imports are estimated at near 500,000 tons, most from the United States. Iranian soybean oil imports have continued apace, but the U.S. share of the market has decreased.

Jordan (East Bank) is experiencing a third consecutive year of drought, with the wheat crop expected at under 60,000 tons. This will necessitate wheat imports in excess of 250,000 tons.

Israel's wheat crop is expected to be significantly higher in 1977, at around 270,000 tons, up 33 percent from last year. Israel's wheat imports are expected to slacken. Feed grain imports in 1977 will remain unchanged. (*Michael E. Kurtzig: 447-8966*)

In *Syria*, despite good rains during April, moisture conditions earlier in the year were very poor in major grain areas and there could be a sharp drop in the grain production, although the official early estimates indicate production of about 2 million tons for wheat and 200,000 for barley. (*H. Charles Treakle: 447-8966*)

FOOD AND TRADE POLICY DEVELOPMENTS

Conference on International Economic Cooperation

The Conference on International Economic Cooperation (CIEC) held its final session in May 1977. CIEC was formed at the ministerial level in 1975 to carry out a dialogue between developed and developing countries on energy, raw materials, development, and financial affairs. The 8 industrialized and 19 developing countries participating agreed to the establishment of a common fund to help stabilize commodity prices and to a $1-billion special action program to assist individual low-income countries with inadequate economic resources. Secretary of State Cyrus Vance told the participants that the United States would take part in efforts: to establish individual commodity agreements to stabilize prices "wherever the nature of the commodity and the market permits;" "to create

a common fund—that is efficient and that works—to back up commodity agreements;" to assure adequate compensatory financing to developing countries to offset fluctuations in their export earnings; to provide investment for developing new supplies; and to support diversification and product improvement.

The U.S. announced that it is prepared, upon Congressional approval, to contribute $375 million to the special action program. This contribution would be in addition to present levels of bilateral aid to the poorest countries. Considerable disagreement remains among participants concerning the purposes, objectives, and other constituent elements of a common fund. These are to be negotiated further in UNCTAD (United Nations Conference on Trade and Development).

The Conference ended in disagreement over the

indexing of commodity prices and the moratorium on debt repayments—both sought by the developing countries—and over continuing an energy dialogue sought by the industrial nations. Because CIEC is not a negotiating forum, issues discussed at the Conference will be pursued in other international forums such as UNCTAD.

International Fund for Agricultural Development

The International Fund for Agricultural Development (IFAD), proposed by the 1974 World Food Conference to mobilize additional concessional aid for agricultural development in developing countries, may come into operation before the end of 1977. The $1-billion target in pledges has been met and other outstanding issues such as allocation of resources and project supervision and appraisal have been resolved.

Over 90 countries are participating in the establishment of the Fund and almost half, including all the OPEC countries except Kuwait and Venezuela, have signed the agreement. Once notification (the depositing of instruments of cash or credit pledged) has been made by a sufficient number of participating countries, the Fund can become operational. The United States, the largest single donor with a $200-million pledge, is prepared to ratify in concurrence with other major donors.

If a sufficient number of notifications are received by the next session of the IFAD Preparatory Commission in July 1977, the Governing Council could convene in the fall.

IFAD's support will be primarily for projects and programs specially designed to introduce, expand, or improve food production systems and to strengthen related policies and institutions. Priority will be given to countries with per capita incomes of $500 or less (1975 prices), particularly to the poorest, and to small farmers and landless agricultural laborers in all developing countries.

Multilateral Trade Negotiations

Specific goals for 1977 set by the United States and six other major industrial nations at the International Economic Summit Meeting in May should give new impetus to the stalled talks at the Multilateral Trade Negotiations (MTN). Progress to date has been most visible in the Tropical Products Group where Australia, the EC, Finland, New Zealand, Norway, and Switzerland agreed to implement part or all of their trade concessions and contributions on tropical products to developing countries on January 1, 1977. Japan and Canada implemented concessions on April 1 and Austria is expected to implement concessions following parliamentary approval.

The commodities on which developed countries made concessions included coffee, cocoa, tea,

spices, jute, tobacco, sugar and tropical fruits, and some semi-processed and processed products. Most concessions involved unbound duty reductions under the developed countries' Generalized System of Preferences.

The United States has offered trade concessions which when fully implemented would reduce duties on a most-favored-nation basis on almost 150 tropical products, valued at approximately $1 billion, to 41 developing countries. Consultations on the U.S. offer are continuing with developing countries.

Differences in the scope and approach to the treatment of agriculture have generally slowed the progress in other MTN groups. One of the goals for the MTN set in the May 1977 "Downing Street Summit" in London by the United States and six other industrial nations—West Germany, France, the United Kingdom, Italy, Canada, and Japan— was to make substantive progress in 1977 on "a mutually acceptable approach to agriculture that will achieve increased expansion and stabilization of trade and greater assurance of world food supplies." Two others of major importance to agriculture are: (1) a tariff reduction plan of broad application which will substantially cut and harmonize or eliminate tariffs; and (2) codes, agreements, and other measures that will significantly reduce nontariff barriers to trade and will act to avoid new barriers in the future. (*Barbara S. Blair: 447-7590*)

World Food Council Meeting

Secretary Bergland, at a meeting of the World Food Council (WFC) held June 20-24 in Manila, outlined the basic principles guiding the U.S. approach to the question of grain reserves. The U.S. proposals stress the need for: A reserve stock mechanism "designed to reduce wide fluctuations around the long-term trend in market prices," for which the United States is "willing to consider price indicators to trigger reserve action;" the sharing of the cost of reserve stocks among both exporting amd importing nations, with "special provisions...to assist poor nations in meeting their share;" and the prevention of the "interruption in trade for grains which prevent adjustments in consumption and production in times of extreme surplus and scarcity."

Bergland expressed a hope that "the International Wheat Council soon can lay the foundation for negotiations of an agreement which would include a coordinated system of nationally held reserve stocks."

The WFC agreed in principle to the establishment of national grain reserves from currently surplus stocks, and that both importing and exporting countries should bear the costs of creating an international system of food reserves of which the national reserves would be a part. In addition, the

WFC agreed to a proposal for the establishment of an emergency grain reserve of 500,000 tons.

The WFC also agreed to the importance of increasing food production in developing countries, particularly in the "food priority countries," as a long-term solution to world food security. It agreed that a substantial increase in external and internal resources was needed to reach the agreed goal of a 4-percent growth rate in food production by developing countries.

The WFC reaffirmed the target of 10 million tons of cereals as food aid during 1977/78 and recommended that a new Food Aid Convention be developed as part of a new world grain agreement due to be worked out by July 1978. (*Richard Kennedy: 447-8261*)

Japan	Jan.	+0.9	-23.9	-2.3	+23.5	+7.7	+7.8	---	+7.0	---	-38.9	+3.8
West Germany	Sept.	-2.8	+.8	+6.8	+19.2	+2.9	+8.8	+12.1	---	+11.2	+135.2	+9.1
France	Sept.	+15.9	+9.9	+5.9	+19.2	+9.7	+13.1	+17.1	---	+19.7	+260.8	+20.5
Italy	Sept.	+15.7	+41.8	+4.6	+28.3	+12.1	+33.2	+30.8	---	+23.7	+190.8	+22.1
Netherlands	Sept.	+9.2	+2.6	+10.6	+19.7	+7.3	+10.8	---	---	+16.2	+106.2	+10.5
Belgium	Sept.	+3.6	+2.6	+5.5	+32.7	+3.7	+9.0	---	---	+12.5	+131.4	+10.4
United Kingdom	Sept.	+34.0	+4.0	+12.6	+25.9	+7.8	+30.8	---	---	+30.7	+176.7	+27.4
Ireland	Sept.	+38.0	+8.9	+20.1	+37.6	+10.3	+16.2	---	---	+22.7	+27.3	+27.3
Denmark	Sept.	+3.0	+7.8	+14.9	+40.5	+10.0	+9.9	---	---	+17.0	+44.4	+10.9
EC-9	Sept.	+15.0	+7.6	+8.2	+20.6	+10.6	+21.9	+21.3	---	+22.6	+172.5	+18.8

Table 2.—Index of prices received by farmers in selected countries

(1970=100)

Country	1972	1973	1974	1975	1974				1976		
					I	II	III	IV	I	II	III
Australia	119	166	159	150	148	147	149	157	159	159	
Belgium	112	127	126	142	124	136	134	143	156	156	147
Canada	110	165	197	196	189	198	202	194	197		177
Denmark	113	146	148	161	141	158	161	171	179	182	
France	118	133	138	150		145	145	154	161	169	169
Germany	114	122	118	133	120	124	131	140	150	147	146
Ireland	126	163	164	207	192	198	201	228	247	260	
Italy	116	145	171	92	181	181	184	198	217	224	264
Japan	107	132	160	173	170	171	167	188	195		224
Korea	148	164	216	---	241	253	275	294	---		
Netherlands	1	124	117	131	123	126	127	142	151	146	
New Zealand	123	173	156	---	129	132	140	159	166	156	142
Norway	107	113	123	142	129	130	153	157	151		
Portugal	114	130	146	162	152	157	159	180	205	205	
Spain	125	141	153	177	164	182	176	183	191	206	
Sweden	112	123	134	150	143	144	154	159	163		
United Kingdom	114	147	166	205	186	192	201	227	257	262	254
United States	115	156	167	165	154	161	172	171	169	174	173
Yugoslavia	110	124	161	---	188	194	200	202	204		

Source: Adapted from data in Food and Agricultural Organization of the United Nations, Monthly Bulletin of Agricultural Economics and Statistics, May 1976, EC Index of Producer Prices of Agricultural Products, Annual Supplement to Selling Prices of Agricultural Products, 1976.

United States	:May	+9.6	+16.1	+13.7	+8.3	+15.0	+23.9	+.5	+3.9	+8.2	-1.2	+9.9	+6.8
Canada	:Sept.-Dec.	-1.5	---	---	---	---	---	-9.0	---	+15.6	-4.7	---	+4.3
Japan	:Jan.	+1.1	-1.2	-1.8	-.8	-1.4	-1.0	+2.5	-13.5	---	-6.1	---	+6.8
West Germany	:Sept.	+18.3	+15.4	+13.0	+20.8	+5.6	---	+.3	---	---	-2.1	+2.0	-3.0
Italy	:Sept.	---	+34.0	+35.6	+35.2	+36.3	+32.1	---	-0.8	+0.7	---	+32.3	---
Netherlands	:Sept.	---	+18.3	+16.5	+20.4	+16.3	+15.9	---	+8.2	-2.4	---	-3.9	---
Belgium	:Sept.	---	+13.7	+11.9	+12.6	+19.8	+11.3	---	-17.1	-22.6	---	-5.7	+4.0
United Kingdom	:Sept.	+34.6	+41.6	+37.3	+29.7	+35.3	+33.6	+11.0	---	-13.7	---	+32.8	---
Ireland	:July	---	+25.4	---	---	+27.8	+24.9	---	---	---	---	+46.6	---
Denmark	:Sept.	---	---	---	---	+26.9	+28.3	---	---	-9.4	---	+10.5	---

Table 4. Export and Import Unit Values of Selected Commodities Changes
from the Same Month a Year Earlier

Month	United States		Japan	West Germany	Canada
	December	April	January	December	February
	:- - - - - - - - - - - - - - Percent change - - - - - - - - - - - - - - -				
Wheat	-17.9 (X)	-22.7 (X)	-29.7 (I)	-24.9 (I)	-20.6 (X)
Corn	-8.9 (X)	-7.7 (X)	-13.6 (I)	-10.0 (I)	---
Soybeans	+26.0 (X)	+78.9 (X)	+12.5 (I)	+35.4 (I)	+47.3 (I)
Soybean Oil	-11.5 (X)	+45.1 (X)	---	---	+19.5 (I)
Soybean Meal	+21.0 (X)	+46.5 (X)	---	+36.2 (I)	+34.6 (I)
Cotton	+33.4 (X)	+27.2 (X)	+33.8 (I)	+41.6 (I)	+53.6 (I)
Tobacco	+14.0 (X)	+8.9 (X)	---	+8.7 (I)	+2.6 (X)
Rice	-15.1 (X)	+26.2 (X)	---	+8.1 (I)	-18.8 (I)
Coffee	+104.9 (I)	+158.8 (I)	+74.4 (I)	+16.2 (I)	+131.4 (I)
Sugar	-35.3 (I)	-32.3 (I)	-44.6 (I)	-23.9 (I)	-32.6 (I)
Cocoa Beans	+35.3 (I)	+90.2 (I)	+95.7 (I)	+109.8 (I)	+83.5 (I)
Beef	+3.8 (I)	+3.3 (I)	---	-2.9 (I)	-5.2 (X)
Natural Rubber	+35.8 (I)	+20.2 (I)	+28.7 (I)	+12.3 (I)	-13.0 (I)
Export Unit Value Index	0	+12.4	+14.3	+0.7	
Import Unit Value Index	+33.6	+69.9	+0.3	+12.5	-14.2

I = Import, unit value

X = Export, unit value

Table 5.--The food component of the consumer price index in selected countries

Country	1972	1973	1974	1975	1975 I	1975 II	1975 III	1975 IV	1976 I	1976 II	1977 III	1977 IV
								1970=100				
Argentina	231	359	413	1,187	575	711	1,384	2,079	3,372	6,076	7,279	9,802
Australia	108	124	143	154	148	153	155	160	168	169	174	
Austria	110	118	128	136	133	135	139	139	142	143	146	140
Bangladesh	148	147	248	300	347	299	291	264	241	234	248	245
Belgium	109	117	128	143	136	140	145	150	156	159	160	164
Cameroon	114	123	146	171	166	167	175	176	179	186	188	
Canada	109	125	145	164	156	160	169	170	168	168	169	168
Colombia	128	169	215	281	272	298	276	279	301	316	334	364
Czechoslovakia	99	100	100	100	100	100	100	100	100	100		
Denmark	116	131	147	163	158	163	168	164	172	179	181	191
Ecuador	118	142	188	223	219	224	222	229	233	234	256	
Egypt	106	140	135	152	144	150	151	162	163	174		
Ethiopia	88	99	108	113	103	110	117	121	133	162	168	176
France	115	126	141	158	149	154	158	162	166	170	174	180
Germany, West	110	118	124	130	127	131	131	131	135	138	137	137
Greece	109	133	169	189	184	190	183	200	212	219	209	221
India	108	131	171	179	182	183	179	171	153	151	158	162
Indonesia	113	162	229	277	259	268	278	302	324	329	345	352
Iran	116	124	144	161	165	176	154	149	166	181		
Ireland	120	140	160	195	183	201	195	201	213	226		
Israel	123	149	215	314	298	314	308	338	353	387	408	460
Italy	111	124	146	172	166	170	174	179	187	199	204	217
Japan	110	124	159	180	174	178	180	186	192	196	196	200
Jordan	118	140	189	219	211	226	204	233	285	265	248	269
Korea	135	138	176	233	203	227	244	255	261	270	277	285
Liberia	91	118	149	172	168	171	179	172	168	170		
Malawi	116	124	144	172	166	168	168	185	188	172	169	170
Malaysia	105	121	154	159	162	157	158	159	161	160		
Mexico	109	126	164	184	176	182	189	191	197	200	205	225
Mozambique	130	127	155	---	172	174	174	173	182	191	185	
Netherlands	111	120	129	139	135	137	140	143	147	151	154	158
New Zealand	114	127	142	157	147	153	160	168	175	183	190	196
Niger	123	144	148	160	152	156	164	168	175	193	208	229
Nigeria	126	120	150	214	179	214	228	237	267	265	266	
Pakistan	105	131	171	209	197	211	215	217	212	216	224	235
Paraguay	121	147	183	192	187	183	195	201	203	198	196	202
Peru	115	126	150	199	180	180	196	212	233	237	282	301
Philippines	157	164	237	253	256	250	251	257	271	276		
Poland	100	102	113	114	113	114	114	115	---	---		
Portugal	120	131	173	214	203	211	216	226	250	248	263	294
Rep. of South Africa	112	129	149	171	166	168	174	176	178	180	186	190
Spain	118	132	152	177	168	174	183	184	192	210	216	223
Sri Lanka	108	122	139	150	149	150	150	149	149	149	147	147
Sweden	119	126	134	150	142	146	154	158	162	168	172	173
Thailand	101	122	157	164	160	163	164	168	170	171	172	179
Turkey	127	152	181	235	221	237	236	247	263	271	280	296
United Kingdom	121	139	164	206	188	206	211	219	234	243	246	267
United States	108	123	141	153	149	150	155	157	157	157	158	158
Uruguay	241	489	844	1,442	1,268	1,328	1,459	1,710	1,823	3,788		
Venezuela	109	117	132	151	146	149	152	157	157	161		
Yugoslavia	139	169	196	252	232	249	256	273	273	291	274	293
Zaire	133	155	200	---	220	242	261	319	426			
Zambia	112	119	129	---	137	142	149	151	163	171		

Source: International Labor Office, Bulletin of Labor Statistics.

Table 6 —World total grain production, consumption and net exports

Million metric tons

	1960/61-62/63			1969/70-71/72			1973/74			1974/75			1975/76			1976/77			1977/78		
	Pro-duction	Con-sumption	Net exports	Pro-duction	Con-sumption	Net exports	Pro-duction	Con-sumption	Net exports	Pro-duction	Con-sumption	Net exports	Pro-duction	Con-sumption	Net exports	Pro-duction	Con-sumption	Net exports	Pro-duction	Con-sumption	Net exports
Developed Countries	313.38	297.71	20.23	399.33	372.95	31.42	447.19	398.28	58.29	452.10	412.36	54.28	447.00	371.95	75.45	463.12	377.99	29.07	467.61	388.66	58.50
United States	168.26	139.77	32.72	208.74	169.01	39.26	236.03	178.05	74.87	247.08	142.34	64.63	255.34	155.20	82.62	254.79	154.79	76.65	253.25	164.05	71.05
Canada	22.87	14.24	9.69	32.39	20.13	14.86	34.59	21.42	12.68	29.08	18.94	12.79	35.23	19.83	16.56	20.21	20.21	1.90	35.25	20.10	16.13
EC-9	68.86	89.3	-21.49	91.88	109.20	-16.58	104.40	107.63	-3.23	96.05	114.94	-11.45	112.08	90.13	-11.08	43.02	116.28	-25.3	100.63	1.65	-14.98
Other Western Europe	20.05	24.26	-4.92	28.51	33.34	-4.92	37.14	37.10	-9.26	32.78	34.18	-7.65	40.30	32.62	-4.96	90.13	40.34	-7.74	33.42	41.68	-8.31
South Africa	6.98	4.70	2.20	10.14	7.10	2.47	5.79	8.4	3.72	9.60	8.49	3.41	8.81	1.61	1.61	12.25	8.91	2.98	11.49	8.24	3.20
Japan	15.60	20.97	-5.27	12.70	27.86	-14.42	1.54	30.38	-19.86	12.49	29.81	-18.48	30.24	11.19	-19.40	11.39	31.69	-20.94	10.91	32.1	-21.34
Oceania	10.76	4.42	6.65	14.97	12.70	10.75	17.74	6.80	9.37	18.87	5.67	16.89	18.57	5.49	18.57	5.78	3.78	20.64	6.3	12.75	
Centrally Planned Countries	293.38	297.33	-3.27	399.58	414.83	-5.91	465.91	466.53	-15.65	454.06	475.61	-13.54	447.00	490.16	-34.31	493.44	-22.57	475.95	490.31	-20.25	
Eastern Europe	56.58	63.50	-6.64	73.80	81.60	-6.80	85.71	90.1	-4.83	89.70	97.06	-8.35	86.62	91.80	-7.68	101.73	-11.77	91.40	100.46	-8.95	
USSR	126.3	119.01	7.30	167.44	171.82	3.96	211.88	202.03	-5.17	184.78	194.29	-.51	133.35	1.3	-25.40	203.42	-7.75	208.31	200.56	-5.25	
P.R. China	110.89	114.82	-3.93	138.34	161.41	-3.07	168.32	173.97	-3.65	179.58	184.26	-4.68	182.91	184.14	-1.23	188.29	-3.05	183.24	189.29	6.05	
Developing Countries	233.48	244.20	-13.44	307.19	324.3	-18.42	324.10	1.28	-27.42	313.84	348.91	-35.04	348.1	361.08	-31.50	378.95	-24.00	358.65	387.93	-26.25	
Middle America	9.65	10.43	-.90	15.79	16.96	-1.01	17.41	20.40	-3.67	16.46	21.08	-4.94	22.3	19.82	-3.1	23.21	-2.80	19.39	23.34	-3.64	
Venezuela	1.52	1.90	-.39	.84	1.76	-.95	.64	1.94	-1.34	.75	1.90	-1.14	.96	.95	-1.28	2.79	-1.87	1.21	3.23	-2.02	
Brazil	3.83	3.69	-1.84	20.37	22.00	-.83	23.20	24.56	-1.21	19.99	23.32	-1.08	27.1	27.1	-2.1	28.61	-.85	29.1	29.27	.39	
Argentina	3.17	8.26	3.18	1.25	8.05	8.05	24.70	1.37	10.38	19.99	25.79	7.90	21.21	10.30	28.19	-.85	23.28	12.95	1.3	
Other South America	3.63	6.48	-1.04	6.79	8.94	-2.1	6.97	9.87	-2.90	7.41	9.63	-2.25	7.89	10.41	-2.91	7.94	-2.45	8.23	10.87	-2.57	
North Africa/Middle East	1.30	36.1	-5.48	39.62	48.58	-9.07	36.37	50.99	-12.81	42.09	55.80	-15.02	58.40	10.30	-1.66	62.72	-12.89	64.79	25.74	-13.93	
Central Africa	17.38	19.3	-2.07	22.3	8.610	-1.75	18.98	21.3	-2.42	21.3	13.53	-1.94	22.56	7.94	22.49	-2.97	22.3	10.75	-3.3	
East Africa	92.08	97.41	-6.21	119.09	17.82	13.1	10.36	10.39	4.3	81.80	102.15	4.8	161.75	10.98	10.3	138.1	-6.80	134.16	141.19	-5.02	
South Asia	17.34	3.41	3.95	22.91	19.77	-5.1	136.69	136.69	-7.18	43.28	129.73	-9.24	136.42	16.76	133.1	17.3	4.10	122.92	17.56	4.60	
Southeast Asia	23.66	27.88	-4.25	30.39	37.96	-8.20	23.58	20.80	3.42	19.3	16.25	2.97	21.3	21.21	138.1	21.21	-11.72	36.20	48.24	-11.90	
East Asia							32.77	40.92	-10.02	30.3	43.28	-9.66	34.84	4.62	46.85						
Rest of World	6.53	7.43	-.90	6.89	9.70	-2.20	7.39	10.02	-2.27	13.10	15.06	-1.96	13.62	15.88	-2.26	14.00	16.34	-2.34	1.83	16.77	—
Total Above	847.17	846.67	—	1,112.99	1,122.01	—	1,244.59	1,226.10	—	1,193.36	1,199.79	—	1,216.71	1,203.55	—	1,328.36	1,266.72	—	1,316.04	1,283.67	—
World Total	847.90	845.60	—	1,119.80	1,131.50	—	1,251.50	1,245.50	—	1,199.70	1,211.30	—	1,223.20	1,216.80	—	1,335.70	1,279.80	—	1,320.80	1,291.80	—

Table 7 —World wheat production, consumption and net exports

Million metric tons

	1960/61-42/63			1969/70-71/72			1973/74			1974/75			1975/76			1976/77			1977/78		
	Pro-duction	Con-sumption	Net exports	Pro-duction	Con-sumption	Net exports	Pro-duction	Con-sumption	Net exports	Pro-duction	Con-sumption	Net exports	Pro-duction	Con-sumption	Net exports	Pro-duction	Con-sumption	Net exports	Pro-duction	Con-sumption	Net exports
Developed Countries	94.22	74.34	21.27	112.04	87.81	28.38	127.63	85.92	45.3	132.27	85.75	43.56	138.15	84.21	48.72	147.55	87.95	41.43	139.81	91.20	42.72
United States	3.38	16.3	18.14	40.03	21.99	17.38	46.40	20.63	32.82	48.88	19.07	27.3	58.08	20.1	1.60	58.43	21.04	25.39	55.10	23.90	26.90
Canada	12.40	3.96	9.46	13.90	4.67	1.56	16.16	4.60	13.30	13.30	4.61	10.74	17.08	12.25	4.83	13.52	4.88	12.00	16.80	3.00	12.50
EC-9	29.80	3.99	-7.1	36.86	40.88	-3.1	41.39	39.99	-.07	45.39	40.68	2.27	38.10	37.91	2.47	39.58	40.08	.06	41.80	39.88	.50
Other Western Europe	8.46	10.54	-2.07	9.88	10.70	-.71	9.37	9.40	-.87	11.31	10.82	.17	10.40	10.69	.10	11.30	11.12	.17	10.87	1.16	-.20
South Africa	1.78	1.92	-.3	1.46	.66	-.66	1.87	1.56	-.42	1.60	1.04	1.04	1.79	1.74	.03	2.13	1.73	.22	2.00	1.80	-.20
Japan	1.65	4.25	-2.68	.56	3.75	4.70	.20	3.59	-5.32	.23	3.57	-5.38	3.78	3.89	12.38	.22	5.78	-5.46	.24	3.81	-5.61
Oceania	7.75	2.37	3.68	9.35	3.04	8.32	12.24	4.1	6.74	11.56	3.36	8.39	12.46	3.1	8.16	12.38	3.32	8.98	13.00	3.65	8.43

Table 8. World Coarse Grain Production, Consumption and Net Exports

Million metric tons

	1960/61-62/63 Production	Consumption	Net exports	1969/70-71/72 Production	Consumption	Net exports	1973/74 Production	Consumption	Net exports	1974/75 Production	Consumption	Net exports	1975/76 Production	Consumption	Net exports	1976/77 Production	Consumption	Net exports	1977/78 Production	Consumption	Net exports
Developed Countries	204.63	209.16	-1.59	271.75	270.89	.98	303.96	296.43	12.23	263.81	260.65	8.78	296.46	274.13	25.16	299.62	276.51	10.49	312.60	284.01	13.49
United States	133.00	122.52	13.59	165.83	145.80	20.22	186.59	156.05	40.45	150.47	121.79	35.09	184.93	133.70	49.28	193.08	132.39	49.00	194.90	138.70	42.00
Canada	10.47	10.24	.27	18.49	15.41	3.25	18.43	16.76	1.33	15.79	14.28	2.10	18.15	14.94	4.36	19.50	15.28	3.96	18.45	15.04	3.69
EC-9	38.51	52.61	-14.15	54.36	67.59	-12.99	62.23	75.06	-13.00	40.69	73.37	-13.93	57.23	73.35	-13.45	49.90	75.35	-25.20	60.07	74.90	-15.58
Other Western Europe	11.19	13.29	-2.17	18.22	22.13	-4.12	19.29	27.42	-8.31	21.85	28.89	-7.74	21.97	29.13	-6.90	20.94	28.70	-7.79	22.14	30.00	-8.00
South Africa	6.20	3.74	2.38	8.68	5.69	+2.60	11.92	6.78	+3.40	9.66	6.78	3.44	7.80	6.98	1.67	10.13	7.09	2.78	9.49	6.86	3.08
Japan	2.34	4.75	-2.42	.74	11.06	-10.27	.29	13.78	-14.11	1.29	13.32	-13.12	.27	13.76	-13.50	.25	15.11	-15.45	.28	15.90	-15.71
Oceania	2.92	2.01	.91	5.43	3.21	2.29	5.21	2.58	2.47	5.06	2.22	2.94	6.11	2.27	3.70	5.82	2.39	3.19	7.27	2.61	4.01
Centrally Planned Countries	138.48	137.37	.73	177.94	181.73	-3.34	212.16	219.82	-8.61	216.19	221.66	-7.29	185.86	205.25	-19.17	233.96	238.89	-9.89	214.70	227.24	-8.36
Eastern Europe	39.62	40.59	-1.01	47.42	50.25	-2.71	54.10	55.16	-1.01	55.52	60.83	-5.13	58.05	61.00	-3.74	57.00	62.98	-6.94	57.70	63.29	-5.41
USSR	58.97	56.17	2.46	73.81	74.68	-.54	100.95	105.55	-5.60	99.69	99.42	-1.73	65.82	82.37	-15.55	114.96	113.96	-3.00	95.00	102.00	-3.00
P.R. China	39.89	40.61	-.72	56.71	56.80	-.09	57.11	59.11	-2.00	60.98	61.41	-.43	61.99	81.88	-.12	62.00	61.95	-.05	62.00	61.95	.05
Developing Countries	99.39	96.09	2.84	129.05	124.12	5.29	135.97	131.36	3.32	131.79	132.86	-1.14	143.04	139.90	.85	147.96	144.61	2.94	149.46	147.02	2.97
Middle America	7.78	8.00	-.31	13.02	13.25	-.11	14.57	16.07	-2.04	13.16	16.53	-3.27	15.97	17.65	-2.38	15.64	18.13	-1.86	16.45	18.63	-2.06
Venezuela	.47	.52	-.05	.70	.94	-.26	.46	1.18	-.74	.56	1.15	-.67	.72	1.33	-.64	.97	1.79	-1.03	.97	1.97	-1.00
Brazil	9.77	9.60	.18	14.38	14.62	-.39	16.85	15.86	1.29	16.92	16.21	.91	18.45	16.79	1.46	19.61	17.47	1.94	20.61	17.57	2.94
Argentina	7.91	4.68	3.29	13.32	6.70	6.39	14.44	6.06	8.13	13.79	4.18	6.05	12.44	6.52	4.63	16.78	7.90	8.23	17.57	8.15	7.73
Other South America	2.77	2.87	-.05	3.47	3.99	-.39	3.99	4.47	-.29	3.68	4.18	-.44	4.09	4.43	-1.32	3.91	4.28	-.40	4.18	4.18	-.22
North Africa/Middle East	13.90	14.47	-.59	16.38	17.76	-1.22	14.44	16.92	-2.35	17.92	19.66	-2.52	18.39	20.46	-2.32	20.94	22.69	-2.25	20.34	23.32	-2.62
Central Africa	16.25	16.26	-.01	18.79	18.87	-.02	15.71	16.09	-.40	16.92	17.92	-.40	18.52	18.77	.24	18.48	18.83	-.37	18.65	19.02	-.38
East Africa	7.11	6.88	.23	9.12	9.05	-.08	9.87	9.51	.73	9.26	9.33	-.36	10.08	9.83	-.67	9.89	9.58	-.36	9.89	9.63	-.31
South Asia	27.29	27.03	-.14	30.91	31.02	-.10	32.50	32.69	-.84	28.87	29.81	-1.30	33.48	32.70	-2.52	31.46	31.46	-.02	31.46	31.46	-.02
Southeast Asia	5.20	5.59	.19	2.35	2.56	1.77	2.80	.65	2.15	2.98	.70	2.30	3.55	3.91	2.13	3.26	1.26	2.15	3.96	1.26	2.68
East Asia	6.37	7.72	-.46	6.37	7.72	-1.55	6.84	8.90	-2.83	7.19	9.80	-2.83	7.35	10.49	-3.85	7.22	11.08	-3.81	7.09	11.64	-4.39
Rest of World	2.06	2.17	-.11	1.82	2.00	-.18	1.86	2.34	-.48	2.27	2.47	-.20	2.66	2.78	-.13	2.66	2.78	-.13	2.46	2.67	-.22
Total Above	444.56	444.79	--	580.56	578.74	--	653.95	651.95	--	614.06	617.64	--	628.02	622.06	--	684.20	662.79	--	679.22	660.94	--
World Total	444.60	444.80	--	587.30	588.20	--	660.90	665.30	--	620.40	625.00	--	634.50	635.20	--	691.40	673.70	--	684.30	664.60	--

Table 9. World Milled Rice Production, Consumption, and Net Exports

	1960/61-62/63			1969/70-71/72			1973/74			1974/75			1975/76			1976/77			1977/78		
	Pro-duction	Con-sumption	Net exports	Pro-duction	Con-sumption	Net exports	Pro-duction	Con-sumption	Net exports	Pro-duction	Con-sumption	Net exports	Pro-duction	Con-sumption	Net exports	Pro-duction	Con-sumption	Net exports	Pro-duction	Con-sumption	Net exports
									Million metric tons												
Developed Countries	14.3	14.22	.54	15.47	14.60	1.72	15.59	13.96	1.58	16.30	13.82	2.42	17.50	13.62	1.56	15.94	13.3	2.07	15.50	13.45	2.29
United States	1.88	.95	.98	2.88	1.66	1.27	3.04	1.3	1.60	3.67	1.48	2.21	4.08	1.39	1.74	3.82	1.37	2.26	3.25	1.45	2.1
Canada		.04	-.04		.05	-.05		.07	-.07		.06	-.06		.06	-.10		.06	-.06		.06	-.06
EC-9	.3	.75	-.21	.66	.74	-.07	.77	.81	-.16	.76	.73	-.21	.73	.82	-.10	.66	.85	-.22	.76	.67	-.1
Other Western Europe	.40	.43	-.04	.43	.47	-.04	.43	.52	-.12	.40	.47	-.06	.41	.49	-.09	.38	.52	-.12	.41	.52	-.1
South Africa		.06	-.04		.07	-.04		.10	-.08		.07	-.08		.09	-.09		.08	-.08		.08	-.08
Japan	11.61	11.97	-.16	11.3	11.54	-.16	11.06	11.02	.25	11.19	10.92	.01	11.98	10.70	-.02	10.71	10.60	-.02	10.71	10.60	-.02
Oceania	.09	.04	.05	.19	.07	.14	.29	.09	.16	.28	.09	.20	.30	.07	.25	.37	.07	.1	.37	.07	.1
Centrally Planned Countries	52.07	51.79	.29	72.86	72.43	.44	78.10	76.37	1.70	82.97	82.03	.94	82.38	82.01	.38	81.68	81.1	.3	81.40	81.48	.25
Eastern Europe	.08	.25	-.16	.14	.37	-.22	.14	.34	-.22	.1	.3	-.22	.1	.39	-.23	.3	.41	.14	.3	.3	-.40
USSR	.1	.33	-.18	.83	1.10	-.28	1.15	1.21	-.06	1.24	1.52	-.28	1.3	1.56	-.25	1.3	1.56	-.25	1.1	1.56	-.25
P.R. China	51.84	51.21	.63	71.89	70.96	.94	76.81	74.82	1.98	81.60	80.16	1.44	80.92	80.06	+.86	80.24	79.34	+.90	80.24	79.34	.90
Developing Countries	91.27	90.88	.17	114.66	115.94	-1.3	120.72	120.72	-2.69	113.20	117.07	-3.25	128.09	124.88	-.50	122.06	126.60	-2.06	125.37	128.06	-2.05
Middle America	.50	.54	-.04	.71	.81	-.09	.81	.90	-.1	.87	.98	-.20	1.09	1.04	-.3	.77	1.08	-.12	.59	.63	-.04
Venezuela	.06	.06	-.01	.3	.11	.02	.18	.16	.06	.19	.17	.07	.24	.20	.03	.18	.25	-.10	.24	.26	-.02
Brazil	3.78	3.45	.07	4.12	4.00	.09	4.41	4.47	.01	4.76	4.46	-.04	5.78	4.97	.18	4.90	5.19	-.32	3.20	3.40	-.10
Argentina	.1	.09	.02	.21	.15	.07	.13	.08	.06	.23	.13	.06	.20	.20	.08	.14	.14	.16	.20	.1	.05
Other South America	1.74	1.76	-.02	1.41	1.61	-.09	1.61	1.34	.27	1.96	1.58	.3	2.64	1.80	.24	2.07	1.96	.16	2.25	2.10	.10
North Africa/Middle East	2.00	2.36	-.36	2.81	2.70	-.52	2.47	3.08	-.64	2.44	3.29	-.95	2.64	3.3	-.85	2.80	3.79	-1.10	2.95	4.00	-1.05
Central Africa	.1	.3	-.01	2.71	3.22	-.52	2.72	3.42	-.74	2.92	3.50	-.59	3.14	3.73	-.56	3.1	3.96	-.90	4.00	4.05	-1.05
East Afr ch	.1	.3	-.01	.19	.20	-.01	.22	.22	-.02	.28	.29	-.02	.1	.42	-.1	.32	.38	-.07	3.00	4.05	-.07
South Asia	47.1	48.27	-.96	58.05	58.63	-.65	61.00	59.66	.34	56.23	58.18	-.06	67.42	63.49	-.19	61.46	63.24	+.14	64.20	64.20	-.20
Southeast Asia	16.40	13.01	3.39	20.52	18[.]99	+1.91	20.75	19.87	.67	16.29	15.29	.84	17.74	1.67	2.34	17.89	16.16	2.12	17.89	16.20	2.12
East Asia	18.25	20.3	-2.02	23.80	26.02	-2.52	25.82	27.47	-2.1	27.03	29.09	-2.69	27.38	29.88	-1.3	28.34	30.57	-2.64	29.03	30.85	-1.99
Rest of World	4.25	4.43	.02	4.76	4.94	-.18	5.16	5.18	-.03	10.46	10.38	.08	10.60	10.84	-.34	10.98	11.29	-.42	11.00	2.00	---
Total Above	162.12	161.32	---	207.75	207.91	---	219.05	216.23	---	222.93	223.30	---	238.57	231.35	---	230.66	232.75	---	233.55	234.91	---
World Total	162.10	161.30	---	207.90	207.50	---	219.00	216.70	---	222.90	223.40	---	238.60	231.70	---	230.70	232.90	---	233.60	234.90	---

Western Europe	60.6	85.6	92.0	93.8	94.1	91.2	95.8	96.9
Japan	3.5	9.3	11.6	12.6	11.6	11.8	13.3	13.9
II. Central Planned Countries	77.5	143.8	164.4	168.8	176.6	157.9	177.0	182.5
Eastern Europe	28.8	46.5	58.5	55.5	61.8	60.1	61.5	62.0
U.S.S.R.	40.7	84.3	93.9	99.3	100.8	82.8	101.5	105.5
People's Republic of China	8.0	13.0	12.0	14.0	14.0	15.0	14.0	15.0
III. Developing Countries	17.3	29.5	32.0	35.8	36.0	39.9	41.8	42.5
Mexico/Central America	.8	3.0	3.1	4.3	4.6	4.9	5.1	5.2
South America	10.8	17.6	18.1	21.7	20.0	20.0	20.6	20.9
Argentina	3.6	5.2	5.8	6.4	5.3	5.4	5.7	6.0
North Africa/Middle East	4.5	5.9	6.1	5.3	6.6	9.1	10.2	10.0
Other Developing Africa	.1	.1	.1	.1	.1	.1	.1	.1
South Asia	.4	.7	1.1	1.3	1.1	1.4	1.2	1.1
India	.3	.6	.7	1.0	.7	1.0	.9	.8
Southeast Asia	--	.1	.2	.2	.3	.4	.5	.7
Thailand	--	.1	.2	.2	.3	.4	.5	.7
East Asia	.7	2.1	3.3	2.9	3.3	4.0	4.1	4.5
IV. Rest of World	--	--	--	--	--	--	--	--
Total Above								
V. World Total (million metric tons)	282.7	425.4	470.6	477.1	445.0	439.2	465.6	481.7

Table 11—World Grain Carryover

Country/Region	1960/61–62/63	1969/70–71/72	1972/73	1973/74	1974/75	1975/76	1976/77	1977/78
				1,000 metric tons				
I. Developed Countries	143,371	126,872	87,401	77,328	73,800	78,514	108,622	130,722
United States	103,129	67,444	48,195	31,305	27,349	36,607	60,502	78,302
Other Developed Exporters	19,556	35,184	18,200	21,880	18,288	17,595	25,180	25,480
Western Europe	18,123	16,938	16,944	19,733	23,366	17,858	17,095	21,195
Japan	2,563	7,306	4,062	4,410	4,797	6,454	5,845	5,745
II. Central Planned Countries	7,597	13,272	13,539	28,578	20,576	10,769	30,064	39,919
Eastern Europe	2,930	3,605	2,539	2,578	3,576	2,769	4,612	4,467
U.S.S.R.	4,667	9,667	11,000	26,000	17,000	8,000	25,452	35,452
People's Republic of China	—	—	—	—	—	—	—	—
III. Developing Countries	16,570	31,066	27,709	31,540	31,596	42,040	48,653	47,153
Mexico/Central America	766	822	598	1,299	1,617	2,285	1,803	1,703
South America	3,353	4,873	3,531	4,380	4,669	5,098	5,886	5,786
Argentina	751	1,323	1,227	2,182	2,201	1,333	2,532	2,032
North Africa/Middle East	2,110	3,533	5,162	6,166	7,477	9,108	12,552	13,552
Other Developing Africa	17	734	1,024	757	832	843	883	883
South Asia	9,082	15,587	13,234	12,849	10,106	18,772	20,869	18,359
India	8,120	14,150	11,100	10,400	7,500	15,950	19,270	14,770
Southeast Asia	362	1,544	902	969	1,073	613	726	726
Thailand	362	1,544	902	969	1,073	613	681	681
East Asia	880	3,973	3,258	5,120	5,822	5,321	5,934	6,134
IV. Rest of World	—	—	—	—	—	—	—	—
Total Above	167,538	171,210	128,649	137,446	125,972	131,323	187,339	217,794
V. World Total (million metric tons)	167.5	174.5	131.8	137.7	126.1	131.6	187.5	205.2

Developed															
United States 5/	25.4	11.6	14.6	34.3	16.1	15.3	27.3	13.9	14.7	33.3	16.7	17.5	27.8	16.4	16.7
Canada	1.3	0.4	0.9	1.3	0.2	0.8	1.2	0.5	0.8	1.5	0.6	0.9	1.1	0.2	0.9
EC-9	1.1	-12.5	13.6	1.2	-13.9	15.1	1.1	-13.5	14.7	1.2	-14.8	16.0	1.0	-14.8	15.8
O.W. Europe	1.0	-1.9	2.9	1.1	-2.3	3.4	1.1	-2.4	3.5	1.1	-2.5	3.7	1.1	-2.7	3.8
Japan	1.0	-2.7	3.8	1.2	-3.6	4.8	1.2	-3.4	4.6	1.2	-3.5	4.7	1.2	-3.7	4.9
Aust. & N. Z.	0.1	-0.1	0.2	0.1	-0.1	0.2	0.1	-0.1	0.2	0.1	-0.1	0.2	0.1	-0.1	0.2
South Africa	0.7	0.4	0.3	0.7	0.1	0.6	0.6	-0.1	0.6	0.6	-0.1	0.6	0.7	-0.1	0.7
Total	30.6	-4.8	36.3	39.9	-3.5	40.2	32.7	-5.0	39.1	39.0	-3.7	43.6	35.6	-4.7	43.0
Central Plan															
East Europe	1.3	-1.2	2.5	1.6	-4.0	5.6	1.5	-4.0	5.5	1.6	-4.2	5.8	1.7	-4.2	5.9
U.S.S.R.	4.5	---	4.5	5.2	-.1	5.3	4.6	-0.2	4.8	4.2	-1.2	5.4	4.2	-1.5	5.7
P. R. China	3.9	0.2	3.7	4.8	-.6	5.4	5.2	---	5.2	5.3	-0.1	5.4	5.3	-0.1	5.4
Total	9.7	-1.0	10.7	11.6	-4.7	16.3	11.3	-4.2	15.5	11.1	-5.5	16.6	11.2	-5.8	17.0
Less Developed															
Mexico & Cent. Am.	0.8	-0.1	0.9	1.0	-.3	1.3	1.0	-0.2	1.2	1.0	-0.4	1.4	0.7	-0.6	1.3
Brazil	1.8	1.1	0.7	5.6	4.2	1.4	7.9	6.3	1.6	8.6	7.1	1.5	9.2	7.7	1.5
Argentina	0.8	0.8	0.2	1.1	0.5	0.5	0.7	0.2	0.5	1.2	0.7	0.5	1.6	1.0	0.5
O. S. America	3.7	2.9	0.8	2.1	0.9	1.3	1.9	0.9	1.0	2.1	1.1	1.0	2.1	1.0	1.1
North Africa	0.7	-0.3	0.4	0.8	0.1	0.7	0.2	0.2	0.6	0.7	0.1	0.6	0.8	0.2	0.6
Central Africa	2.1	1.4	0.7	1.9	0.9	1.0	2.0	1.0	1.0	2.1	1.0	1.1	2.1	1.0	1.1
West Asia	0.7	0.7	0.7	0.9	-0.1	1.0	0.8	-0.1	0.9	0.9	-0.1	1.0	0.9	-0.1	1.0
South Asia	4.2	0.7	3.6	4.6	0.9	3.7	4.3	0.8	3.5	4.6	1.3	3.4	4.5	0.9	3.8
Southeast Asia	0.2	0.1	0.3	0.3	0.0	0.3	0.3	0.3	0.3	0.3	0.3	0.3	0.3	0.3	0.3
East Asia, Pac.	1.5	---	1.6	1.6	0.6	1.0	2.0	0.5	1.5	2.3	0.7	1.6	2.1	0.5	1.6
Total	16.7	7.3	9.6	19.8	8.5	12.2	22.1	9.9	12.1	23.8	11.5	12.4	25.5	11.7	12.6
Grand total	57.0	---	56.6	71.4	---	68.7	66.1	---	66.7	73.9nb	---	72.6	71.7	---	72.5
Grand total less U.S.	31.6	---	42.0	37.1	---	53.5	38.8	---	52.0	40.6	---	56.1	43.9	---	56.5

1/ Oilseed meals include those from soybeans, cottonseed, peanuts, rapeseed, sunflower, linseed, sesame, copra, and palm kernels. Fish-meal data are adjusted by a factor of 1.5 to reflect its higher protein content, none of the other meals was converted.
2/ Preliminary.
3/ Partially forecast.
4/ Forecast.
5/ U.S. disappearance estimates include the effect of stock variations and are based largely on crop year estimates.

Table 13.—World edible vegetable oil production, net trade and availability (oil equivalent basis)
for 1969-71 average, 1974 preliminary 1975, forecast 1976 and 1977 1/

Million metric tons

	1969-71 average			1974 2/			1975 3/			1976 4/			1977 5/		
	Production	Net exports	Disappearance	Production	Net exports	Disappearance	Production	Net exports	Disappearance	Production	Net exports	Disappearance	Production	Net exports	Disappearance
Developed															
United States 5/	6.01	2.22	3.87	7.99	3.10	4.11	6.41	2.28	4.35	7.71	2.49	4.90	6.51	2.78	4.74
Canada	.33	.13	.20	.45	.13	.32	.47	.17	.30	.66	.33	.33	.38	.02	.36
EC-9	.79	-3.06	3.85	.92	-3.16	4.08	.88	-3.62	4.50	1.00	-3.60	4.60	.86	-3.83	4.69
O.W. Europe	.77	-.38	1.15	.93	-.46	1.39	.84	-.51	1.35	.97	-.43	1.40	.87	-.54	1.41
Japan	.03	-.73	.76	.02	-1.04	1.06	.02	-.87	.89	.02	-.92	.94	---	-1.12	1.12
Aust. & N. Z.	.02	-.05	.07	.04	-.06	.13	.04	-.06	.10	.05	-.06	.11	.06	-.06	.12
South Africa	.12	-.03	.09	.21	.08	.13	.13	-.01	.12	.12	---	.12	.13	-.01	.14
Total	8.06	-1.84	9.98	10.54	-1.36	11.18	8.78	-2.61	11.61	10.49	2.33	12.40	9.28	-2.72	12.58
Central Plan															
East Europe	.90	.02	.88	1.05	-.13	1.18	.94	.10	1.04	1.11	.05	1.06	1.12	-.05	1.17
U.S.S.R.	3.08	.51	2.57	3.57	-.51	3.06	3.39	.49	2.90	2.70	-.20	2.95	2.80	-.15	2.95
P. R. China	1.68	.08	1.60	2.06	-.13	2.19	2.33	-.10	2.43	2.36	-.14	2.50	2.38	-.38	2.76
Total	5.66	.61	5.05	6.68	.25	6.43	6.66	.29	6.37	6.16	-.24	6.50	6.30	-.58	6.88
Less Developed															
Mexico & Cent. Am.	.39	-.16	.55	.49	-.26	.75	.53	-.06	.59	.47	-.14	.61	.48	-.19	.67
Brazil	.69	.05	.64	1.69	.54	1.15	1.96	.91	1.05	2.29	1.20	1.17	2.45	1.15	1.30
Argentina	.41	.10	.31	.50	.10	.40	.44	.06	.38	.57	.17	.40	.56	.21	.38
O. S. America	.24	-.12	.36	.29	-.21	.50	.38	-.12	.50	.40	-.12	.52	.37	-.20	.57
North Africa	.48	-.15	.63	.83	-0.1	.84	.87	-.03	.90	.89	-.06	.95	.88	-.11	.99
Central Africa	2.59	.97	1.62	2.44	-.80	1.64	2.57	.62	1.95	2.61	.56	2.05	2.68	-.38	2.30
West Asia	.49	-.21	.70	.65	-.42	1.07	.69	-.49	1.18	.67	-.58	1.25	.65	-.65	1.30
South Asia	2.45	-.13	2.58	2.60	-.34	2.94	2.64	-.24	2.88	2.95	-.21	3.16	2.48	-.52	3.48
Southeast Asia	.13	-.01	.14	.19	---	.19	.19	---	.19	.19	---	.19	.21	-.52	.23
East Asia, Pac.	2.55	1.24	1.31	3.68	2.16	1.52	4.42	2.83	1.59	5.08	3.39	1.69	4.88	2.92	2.06
Total	10.41	1.58	8.83	13.55	2.64	11.01	14.69	3.46	11.23	16.12	4.21	11.99	15.64	3.39	13.28
Grand total	24.12	---	23.87	30.57	---	28.23	30.13	---	28.21	32.77	---	30.89	31.22	---	32.74
Grand total less U.S.	18.11	---	20.00	22.58	---	24.62	23.72	---	24.86	25.06	---	25.99	25.01	---	28.00

1/ Includes soybean oil, cottonseed oil, peanut oil, sunflower, sesame oil, coconut oil, palm oil, palm kernal oil, and olive oil.
2/ Preliminary.
3/ Partially forecast.
4/ Forecast.
5/ U.S. disappearance estimates include the effect of stock variations.

Table 14.--Selected average annual and monthly prices for vegetable oils 1/

Period	Soybean	Peanut	Cottonseed	Rape	Palm	Coconut
Annual						
1970	304	451	392	295	266	358
71	252	418	324	232	215	249
72	465	540	500	395	395	503
73	792	1,091	891	782	686	994
74					.	
75	547	862	720	563	420	394
76	414	857	641	415	405	418
Monthly						
1976						
Oct.	479	753	2/ 620	2/ 460	463	2/ 495
Nov.	488	753	2/ 600	454	460	2/ 494
Dec.	461	n.q.	585	475	454	553
1977						
Jan.	455	849	592	2/ 488	462	546
Feb.	493	856	637	555	507	576
Mar.	584	871	706	610	598	735
Apr.	647	881	735	2/ 695	635	802

n.q. = not quoted.
1/ All are c.i.f. North European ports except soybean oil which is f.o.b. Decatur.
2/ This footnote indicates a change in sources of the oil or in the shipping basis.

Table 15.--World Centrifugal Sugar Production, Trade, and Consumption

Country and Region	Production				Net Exports			Consumption		
	1969/70-71/72 Average	1974/75	1975/76	1976/77	1970-72 Average	1974	1975	1970-72 Average	1974	1975
				- - Thousand metric tons, raw value - -						
North America	17,423	17,147	19,186	18,734	2,265	2,079	3,823	14,997	15,160	14,285
Canada	127	101	120	130	-953	-905	-953	1,055	984	1,057
United States 1/	5,581	5,335	6,535	6,260	-4,941	-5,188	-3,311	10,532	10,290	9,110
Cuba	6,282	5,700	6,200	5,800	5,519	5,491	5,744	569	522	499
Dominican Republic	1,073	1,135	1,249	1,361	982	1,055	975	135	172	166
Mexico	2,466	2,727	2,722	2,700	587	496	207	1,996	2,344	2,558
Other North America	1,894	2,149	2,360	2,483	1,071	1,130	1,161	710	848	875
South America	9,126	12,517	11,380	12,927	2,684	3,740	2,817	7,140	8,313	8,847
Argentina	956	1,532	1,349	1,619	136	644	197	1,012	1,000	1,086
Brazil	5,120	7,400	6,200	7,500	1,666	2,303	1,730	3,806	4,578	4,990
Other South America	3,050	3,585	3,831	3,808	1,108	793	890	2,322	2,635	2,771
Western Europe	10,974	10,636	12,730	13,244	-1,855	-2,683	-2,742	14,220	15,698	13,398
EC-9	9,289	8,977	10,133	10,523	-831	-1,057	-1,474	10,566	11,718	9,562
Other Western Europe	1,685	1,659	2,247	2,721	-1,024	-1,626	-1,268	3,654	3,980	3,836
Eastern Europe	4,255	4,817	5,020	5,514	-471	-446	-476	4,877	5,229	5,296
USSR	8,554	7,730	7,700	7,350	-1,160	-1,739	-3,178	10,449	11,250	11,304
Africa	4,701	5,688	5,477	6,263	491	347	-10	4,393	4,945	5,166
South Africa Republic	1,629	1,883	1,802	2,042	833	826	808	958	1,140	1,215

ugal Sugar Stocks, Beginning of Season 1969/70-1976/77 1/

- - - - - - -Thousand Metric Tons - - - - - - - - - -

60	1,004	1,508	1,710
08	515	1,200	1,584
85	29	28	272
910	1,739	1,649	1,889
681	704	777	737
370	336	370	605
165	522	575	743
125	322	357	719
959	17,400	16,100	17,300

tocks at beginning of grinding seasons.

Service.

Table 17—World coffee production and exportable production

		Production				Exportable	
	:	Average :1969/70–71/72:	1974/75	1975/76	1976/77: 2/	Average :1969/70–71/72:	1974/
	:	― ― ― ― ― ― ― ― ― ― ― ― 1,000 bags (60 kg each) ― ― ―					
Latin America	:	40,552	54,450	48,826	35,750	25,955	39,8
Mexico	:	3,225	3,900	4,200	3,800	1,696	2,1
Guatemala	:	1,897	2,540	2,149	2,482	1,648	2,2
El Salvador	:	2,423	3,300	2,328	2,900	2,268	3,1
Brazil	:	17,450	27,500	23,000	9,500	8,867	19,5
Colombia	:	7,817	9,000	8,500	8,800	6,407	7,4
Africa	:	19,735	20,394	18,389	19,008	18,504	19,0
Angola	:	3,333	3,000	1,200	1,200	3,233	2,8
Ethiopia	:	2,083	2,050	1,900	2,000	1,422	1,3
Ivory Coast	:	4,358	4,500	5,080	5,000	4,295	4,4
Uganda	:	3,067	3,000	2,800	2,700	3,050	2,9
Asia and Oceania	:	5,209	6,238	6,370	6,725	2,646	3,5
India	:	1,417	1,630	1,478	1,767	960	9
Indonesia	:	2,267	2,675	2,865	2,820	1,423	1,7
World	:	65,496	81,082	73,585	61,483	47,105	62,4

1/ Total harvested production less estimated domestic consumption.
2/ Estimate.
Source: Foreign Agricultural Service.

Table 18 --U.S. green coffee imports by country of origin

	1969-1971 Average	1974	1975	1976
	- - - - - - - - 1,000 bags (60 kg. each) - - - - - - - - - - - -			
Latin America	12,890	11,554	13,287	12,463
Mexico	1,092	1,324	1,662	1,869
Guatemala	777	1,096	874	748
El Salvador	586	1,111	1,018	1,045
Brazil	5,496	2,725	3,748	3,092
Colombia	2,558	3,090	3,400	2,688
Ecuador	460	512	693	767
Africa	6,446	6,375	5,698	5,708
Angola	1,409	2,396	1,202	871
Ethiopia	1,047	505	533	703
Ivory Coast	1,060	749	966	1,330
Uganda	922	940	958	941
Asia and Oceania	1,196	1,279	1,233	1,583
India	96	107	258	197
Indonesia	878	942	765	1,082
Other	3	37	70	34
World 1/	20,535	19,245	20,289	19,788

1/ Regional totals may not precisely add to world total because of rounding.

Source: Economic Research Service.

Table 19--World cocoa bean production

Country and region	Average 1969/70-71/72	1974/75	1975/76	1976/77 1/
	- - - - - - - - - - Thousand metric tons - - - - - - - - - -			
Latin America	367.1	474.0	456.2	461.6
Dominican Republic	36.8	30.0	30.0	35.0
Mexico	26.8	32.7	33.0	34.0
Brazil	183.1	266.6	257.4	257.0
Colombia	16.6	25.0	27.0	29.5
Ecuador	59.3	75.0	64.0	80.0
Venezuela	18.7	17.3	19.0	20.0
Africa	1,088.0	1,004.3	1,003.7	868.7
Cameroon	114.6	117.8	96.0	90.0
Ghana	423.4	375.0	397.0	320.0
Ivory Coast	192.9	242.0	231.0	240.0
Nigeria	271.0	213.0	217.0	160.0
Asia and Oceania	41.0	57.5	61.2	65.2
Malaysia	3.5	13.0	16.0	20.0
Papua/N. Guinea	27.1	33.3	34.0	34.0
World	1,496.1	1,535.8	1,521.1	1,414.0

1/ Estimate.

Source: Foreign Agricultural Service.

Table 20--U.S. imports of cocoa beans by country of origin

Country and region	1969-71 average	1974	1975	1976
	- - - - - - - - - - - 1,000 metric tons - - - - - - - - - -			
Latin America	115.6	116.3	122.6	110.4
Brazil	56.6	53.2	74.5	59.5
Dominican Republic	26.2	25.8	22.8	23.9
Ecuador	12.9	20.8	10.5	10.3
Trinidad and Tobago	2.2	2.0	2.6	1.3
Venezuela	2.9	4.5	6.4	2.8
Africa	153.5	94.7	101.6	113.8
Ghana	98.7	56.2	46.2	48.6
Ivory Coast	25.4	13.9	34.0	19.1
Nigeria	27.2	22.4	15.5	43.1
Asia and Oceania	7.4	13.6	12.3	14.9
Papua/N. Guinea	6.1	18.8	11.6	12.6
Other	---	.1	.1	.1
World 1/	276.5	224.6	236.8	239.2

1/ Regional totals may not add to world total because of rounding.

Source: Foreign Agricultural Service.

Table 21--Cotton production, exports, imports and mill consumption in selected regions 1969/70-1976/77

Million 480-lb. bales

	Production				Exports				Imports				Consumption			
	1969/70-71/72 average	1974/75	1975/76	1976/77	1969/70-71/72 average	1974/75	1975/76	1976/77	1969/70-71/72 average	1974/75	1975/76	1976/77	1969/70-71/72 average	1974/75	1975/76	1976/77
U.S.	10.2	11.5	8.3	10.6	3.4	3.9	3.3	5.1	.1	--	.1	.1	8.2	5.9	7.3	6.7
USSR	10.1	12.9	11.6	12.1	2.5	3.6	3.7	3.8	1.0	.7	.5	.4	8.2	9.0	8.7	8.8
China, People's Republic	9.2	11.5	21.0	10.8	.1	.2	.2	.1	.5	.7	.7	.6	9.5	12.3	12.4	12.0
India	5.1	6.0	5.3	4.9	.7	.1	.3	--	.7	--	.2	.8	5.4	6.0	6.2	5.8
Pakistan	2.7	2.9	2.4	1.8	.7	1.1	.4	.1	--	--	--	--	2.0	2.2	2.2	1.8
Brazil	2.8	2.3	1.8	2.2	1.5	.3	.4	.1	--	--	--	--	1.4	1.7	1.9	2.1
Egypt	2.4	2.0	1.8	1.8	1.4	.9	.8	1.0	--	--	--	.1	.9	1.0	1.0	1.0
Turkey	2.0	2.8	2.2	2.2	1.3	.6	2.2	.7	--	--	--	--	.8	1.1	1.3	1.5
Mexico	1.6	2.2	.9	1.0	1.0	.9	.5	.3	--	--	--	--	.7	.7	.8	.8
Central America	.9	1.4	1.3	1.3	.8	1.4	1.2	1.1	--	--	--	--	.1	.2	.2	.1
Sudan	1.1	1.0	.4	.7	1.0	.5	1.0	1.2	--	--	--	--	.7	.1	.1	.1
EC-9	.1	.1	.1	.1	.1	.2	.1	.2	4.4	3.8	4.0	3.5	4.0	3.5	3.6	3.5
Eastern Europe	--	--	--	--	.1	.2	.3	.1	2.7	3.1	3.2	3.3	2.9	3.3	3.3	3.4
Japan	--	--	--	--	--	--	--	--	3.6	3.2	3.2	3.1	3.3	2.6	3.0	2.9
Hong Kong	--	--	--	--	--	--	--	--	.8	.8	1.3	.8	.7	.8	1.0	.8
Taiwan	--	--	--	--	--	--	--	--	.6	.7	1.0	.7	.6	.7	.9	.9
Korea, Republic of	--	--	--	--	--	--	--	--	.5	.7	1.0	.9	.5	.7	.7	1.0
Other	7.3	8.3	7.2	8.0	4.0	3.4	4.4	4.3	3.5	3.6	4.0	3.9	7.1	7.5	7.5	7.8
World	55.5	64.9	54.3	57.5	18.0	17.3	18.8	18.2	18.3	17.3	19.2	16.2	56.4	59.0	62.3	61.0

Source: Foreign Agricultural Service.

ng of season 1969/70-1977/78

SSR	Foreign non- communist	Total exporters	Total importers
1.4	12.0	13.0	8.4
3.1	14.5	14.9	11.0
2.7	17.5	19.5	10.7
2.4	12.9	13.2	9.2
2.3	5.9	11.0	7.8

Table 23.--U.S. Cotton Exports by Destination, :

Country	:	Average 1969/70- 1971/72	:	1974/7!
Japan	:	730		957
Hong Kong	:	100		73
China, Peoples Republic		0		289
China, Republic of (Taiwan)	:	0		384
Korea, Republic of	:	478		628
Indonesia	:	221		72
India		191		--
Bangladesh		0		48
Philippines		136		111
South Vietnam		107		29
European Community	:	(306)		(316)
Italy		75		98
Germany (West)		56		52
France		42		65
United Kingdom		65		38
Other EC		68		63
Switzerland		27		58
Spain		20		58
Poland		30		22
Romania		49		44
Canada	:	261		186
Others		589		471
World		3,245		3,746

1/ Years beginning August 1.
2/ Export bales were, on the average, packed heavier t
of bales shown here does not agree with the net weight
3/ Less than 500 bales.

SOURCE: Foreign Agricultural Service.

Table 24.--World leaf tobacco production in selected countries and regions, average 1969-71 and annual 1974-76

Region and Country	Average 1969-71	1974	1975	1976 1/
			1,000 metric tons 2/	
North America	1,065	1,198	1,234	1,228
United States	819	903	990	961
Canada	107	117	106	82
Mexico	61	67	51	64
Other North America	79	107	87	121
South America	341	426	500	472
Brazil	193	225	286	258
Argentina	60	98	97	93
Colombia	44	41	58	54
Other South America	44	62	59	67
Western Europe	242	262	328	347
EC-9	401	156	180	176
Greece	84	81	118	139
Spain	22	22	27	28
Other Western Europe	2	3	3	4
Eastern Europe	320	344	415	450
Bulgaria	115	140	162	165
Poland	82	65	102	100
Yugoslavia	44	59	70	83
Other Eastern Europe	79	80	81	102
U.S.S.R.	255	313	298	310
Asia	2,053	2,400	2,279	2,422
People's Republic of China	771	984	960	980
India	353	462	363	347
Turkey	154	204	201	316
Japan	158	151	166	179
Indonesia	112	78	66	63
Pakistan 3/	486	106	118	116
Philippines	87	88	66	83
South Korea	60	96	104	112
Thailand	44	56	66	66
Other Asia	153	174	169	160
Africa	194	219	250	253
Rhodesia	64	79	95	85
South Africa	34	26	28	34
Malawi	20	27	35	38
Other Africa	74	88	92	94
Oceania	20	19	19	19
Australia	16	16	16	16
New Zealand	4	3	3	3
World total	4,491	5,180	5,323	5,501

Note: Details may not precisely add to totals because of rounding.

1/ Estimated.
2/ Farm-sales weight.
3/ Includes Bangladesh.

Source: Foreign Agricultural Service; Economic Research Serive, and U.S. Agricultural Attache Tobacco reports.

Table 25.--U.S. exports of unmanufactured tobacco by major destination,
average 1969-71 and annual 1974-76

Country of Destination	Average 1969-71	1974	1975	1976 1/
	— — — — — — — 1,000 Metric tons 2/ — — — — — — — —			
Japan	18	50	37	60
European Community	(143)	(134)	(125)	(107)
United Kingdom	48	43	36	33
West Germany	45	44	41	33
Italy	10	11	14	15
Netherland	16	14	14	11
Denmark	8	6	8	4
Ireland	5	5	4	4
Belgium-Luxembourg	7	7	4	3
France	4	4	4	4
Switzerland	10	10	12	11
Egypt	1	6	5	5
Sweden	7	7	7	6
Thailand	10	9	9	10
Philippines	3	5	6	7
Australia	6	9	7	5
Taiwan	4	11	7	6
Malaysia	4	5	3	3
New Zealand	2	2	2	2
Sub-Total	208	248	220	222
Other Countries	28	48	35	40
World Total	236	296	255	262

NOTE: Individual items may not precisely add to totals because of rounding.
1/ Preliminary.
2/ Declared weight.

SOURCE: Foreign Agricultural Service and Economic Research Service.

WAS-13   **JULY 1977**

Each spring, ERS reports on the situation and outlook for ;
would like to receive any of this year's reports, or be placed
check the appropriate block(s) below and return this she
Room 0054, South Building, U.S. Department of Agriculture

Current report   Mailing list

[ ]   [ ]

[ ]   [ ]

[ ]   [ ]

[ ]   [ ]

[ ]   [ ]

[ ]   [ ]

[ ]   [ ]

Name and address (include zipcode)